A garden in my life

A garden in my life

by Cynthia Ramsden

Second Edition

Profits will be donated to the charities supported by the National Gardens Scheme;
and to the Oesophageal Patients Association.

FANSHAWE GATE HALL

g

First published in hardback in 2001 by Grafika Limited
Copyright © Cynthia Ramsden and Nicola Ball 2001

Second Edition published in paperback in 2009
Copyright © Cynthia Ramsden and Nicola Ball 2009

A catalogue record for this book is available from the British Library
ISBN 978-0-9541089-2-2

Printed and bound in Great Britain

Grafika Limited
Riverside Studio, Riverside Business Park,
Buxton Road, Bakewell, Derbyshire DE45 1GS
www.grafika-uk.com

Further copies of this book can be ordered online at
www.fanshawegate.com

To my husband John; my children Nicola, Louise, Mark, James, and Anna;
and my grandchildren Rachel, Clare, Harry, Alexander,
Frances, Eleanor, Flora, Matthew and Samuel.

Preface to the Second Edition

This edition of 'A Garden in my Life' is essentially a reprinting in paperback of the original hardback book, which sold out soon after its publication in 2001.

There are only two small, but significant, changes from the original book. The first is the addition of one more grandson, Samuel, who was born in 2003 and takes his place alongside my other grandchildren in the dedication above. The second change is a correction to my recipe for fruit cake on page 146: the omission of flour from the recipe was quickly discovered as readers started to query whether Aunt Bea's famously soggy cake was really so liquid. I am glad to have the opportunity to put that right.

Otherwise, apart from changes to the cover, the book stands as it was first printed. I hope that readers of my second book, 'Garden Tales', will enjoy this account of my first forty years at Fanshawe Gate Hall, and the creation of a much-loved garden.

Fanshawe Gate

Illustration by Charles Ashmore from
'Chantrey Land' (Harold Armitage, pub. 1910).

contents

Daphne Foulsham, Chairman of the National Gardens Scheme, with Cynthia Ramsden at Fanshawe Gate, August 2000.

foreword

To stroll through a beautiful garden with its owner is a particular joy. I had the great pleasure of doing just that with Cynthia Ramsden one balmy afternoon last summer. Imagine my delight when Cynthia told me that she was writing a book, an account of one woman's pleasure in creating her garden. Now we can all enjoy her reminiscences of its progression since 1959 when, as a young mother, she immediately knew she would be dispensing with dahlias and bedding out and turning to a softer planting scheme more in harmony with her 16th century house.

Cynthia has always received full support from her husband, John, and the strong ties of her family are never far from her pen. Her grandfather's formal terraces and ordered vegetable garden, Uncle Jack's lemon trees, and the innovative efforts of her own family all add to the richness of this book.

Since 1995 Cynthia and John have most generously opened Fanshawe Gate Hall for the National Gardens Scheme and the charities it supports, and for Macmillan Cancer Relief.

Suddenly, four years ago, Cynthia was diagnosed as having oesophageal cancer and there were urgent and unknown challenges ahead. After surgery, Cynthia is convinced that her sure and steady path back to health was greatly due to the restorative effects of working quietly in her beloved garden. I am delighted by the revelations in the final chapter that new ideas and projects for this wonderful garden continue to flourish.

Daphne Foulsham
Chairman, National Gardens Scheme
June 2001

Introduction

The garden at Fanshawe Gate Hall has been opened under the National Gardens Scheme since 1995. It is now one of the most visited private gardens in Derbyshire, and is listed in the 'Good Gardens' guide. The garden contains both traditional and modern planting schemes, inspired by the history of the house and its distinctive stone architecture.

Records of Fanshawe Gate Hall date from 1260, but the present buildings are largely of the 16th century. At that time, the Fanshawe family had risen to national prominence as government officials and diplomats. Henry Fanshawe became Remembrancer of the Exchequer to Queen Elizabeth I in 1566, and the same post was held under subsequent monarchs by no fewer than eight other members of the Fanshawe family. The memoirs of Lady Ann Fanshawe (whose mother was born at Fanshawe Gate Hall) have given historians a first hand account of the English Civil War. She married her second cousin, Sir Richard Fanshawe, who was a senior official at the court of King Charles I. Following the King's execution in 1649, the Fanshawes were exiled and imprisoned.

Their fortunes revived after the Restoration of Charles II in 1660. Sir Richard Fanshawe became Ambassador to Portugal, having helped to arrange Charles II's marriage to Catharine of Braganza.

The Fanshawe family gravitated to the south of England. Succeeding generations of the family pursued distinguished careers in the Army, the Navy, the Church, academic life and the Colonial Service. Fanshawe Gate Hall was retained as a tenanted farm. The last Fanshawe known to have lived there was Althea Fanshawe, in the 1740s. At some time in the late 16th or early 17th centuries the house was much reduced, stone and timber being carried a mile away to build Woodthorpe Hall. In 1944 the Fanshawes sold the house to Roy Genders, a former Worcestershire County cricketer and gardening writer. His book 'I Bought a Farm' (pub. 1948 by The Worcester Press) describes the experience of Derbyshire farming in the late 1940s, with Fanshawe Gate Hall disguised as 'Holly Gate Farm'. The house was owned by one other family, the Marrians, before the Ramsdens bought it in 1959.

fanshawe gate hall

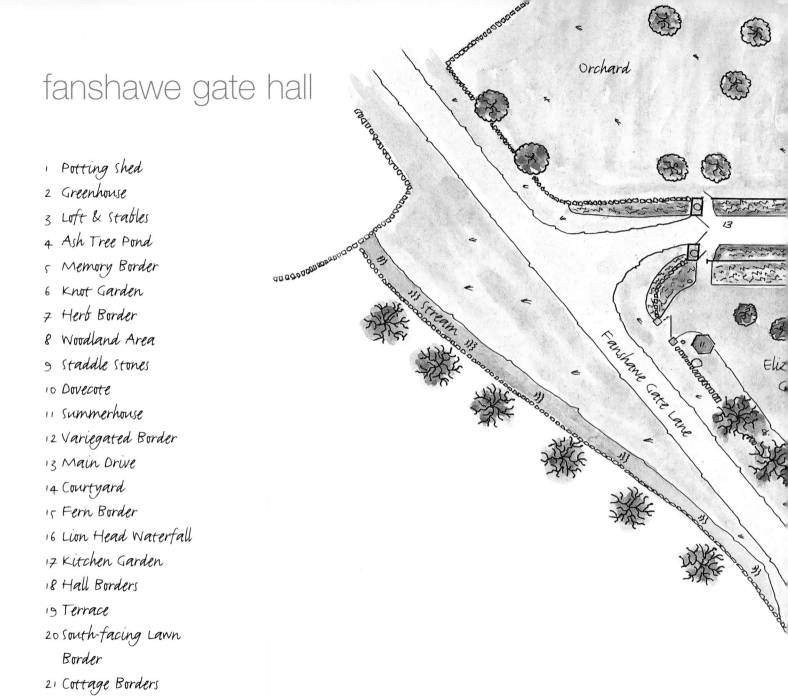

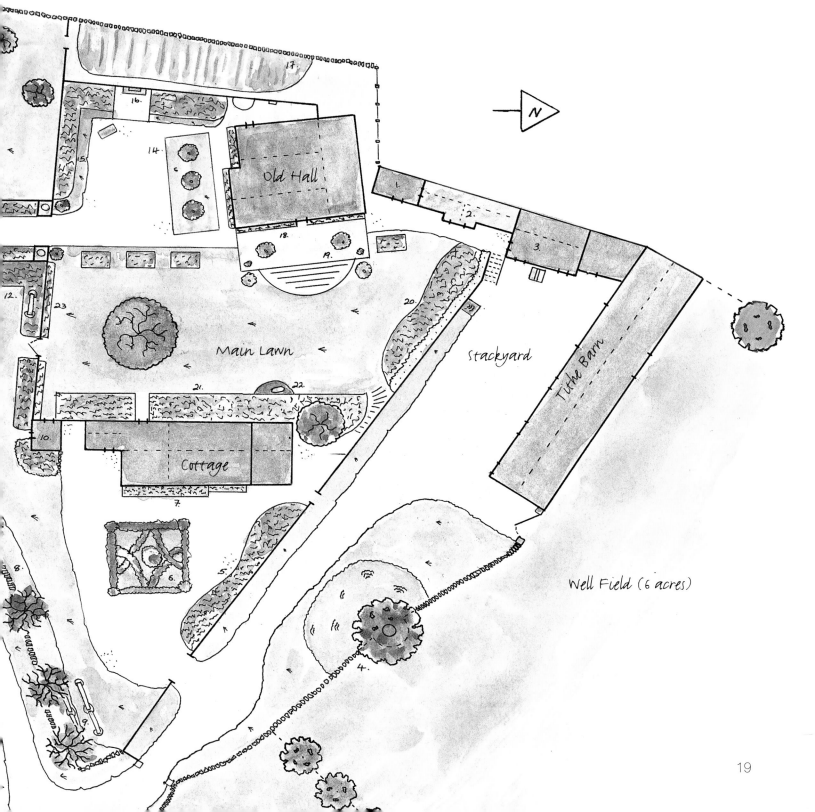

Old Hall

N

Main Lawn

Cottage

Stackyard

Tithe Barn

Well Field (6 acres)

1 from tulips to dahlias

In the 1930s gardens were filled with bedding plants and tulips in neat rows.

In the 1950s Fanshawe Gate Hall was planted largely with multi-coloured dahlias.

How will today's planting choices look to future generations?

Fanshawe Gate Hall in the 1930s.

When Fanshawe Gate Hall was put up for sale in 1959, John and I were living in a modern, clean, centrally heated house in a Sheffield suburb. I still have the sale brochure, with the sepia photograph which so enchanted us. We had one young child and another baby on the way, and we had a romantic vision of where we wanted our children to grow up. The move out to the North Derbyshire village of Holmesfield struck many of our friends as eccentric at the time. Although Holmesfield still had a shop and a post office in those days, and a bus service to Sheffield, Fanshawe Gate Hall was hidden down a remote lane, narrow and steep, which (we were soon to find out) quickly disappears under snowdrifts in winter. The house itself offered damp walls, smoking fireplaces, lethally low wooden beams and an erratic water supply. It was the opposite of our first married home; it was old, dirty and cold, and we absolutely loved it.

Mr Kelk, the tenant farmer at Fanshawe Gate Hall in the early 1900s.

We did know a little about the house, and I would even go so far as to say that we had a sentimental link with its history. Our families have lived in this South Pennine area for generations, and John and I were both pupils in the 1940s at the Dronfield Grammar School. That school was founded in 1579 under the will of Henry Fanshawe, who had become Remembrancer of the Exchequer to Queen Elizabeth I in 1566. The Fanshawe family owned Fanshawe Gate Hall from the 13th century until 1944, when it was sold for the first time. The house changed hands once more in the 1950s, so when we arrived in 1959, we became only the fourth owners in 700 years. My own family also had roots in the village of Holmesfield. When my great-grandmother was born in Gooseberry Cottage, about a mile away from Fanshawe Gate, the old Hall was still in Fanshawe ownership, although occupied by tenant farmers.

This book is really about the garden at Fanshawe Gate, rather than the house, although the restoration of the house has also been a constant theme of our lives. Over time, we have come to feel less like the owners of Fanshawe Gate and more like its guardians or trustees. We have found an increasing sense of commitment to preserve the house, to research its history and to restore both house and garden to their original state; or at least to something which echoes it. Of course we have little evidence to go on, but the four stone gateposts and the gatehouse - the dovecote - suggest that, in the 16th century, a much larger house stood here. What now remains was described by one historian as 'a substantial yeoman's dwelling of Tudor times'.

In fact, the house itself is not very large (and the beams are a continual reminder that Tudor yeomen were not very tall). When our five children were all at home, it was a bit of a squeeze. Now that they have grown up, with children of their own, they have to visit us in shifts or camp out with neighbours. But when the family were young, the size of the house and its ramshackle state did not matter. We spilled out into the garden, and beyond that, into fields and woods. Gardening in those days was little more than holding out against the scorched earth assaults of the children and their pets.

We could always feel the potential of the garden. My first impression of Fanshawe Gate in 1959 was that it was a house which sat perfectly in its garden. The entrance is down a long walled driveway, starting and ending with stone pillars topped by spherical and acorn-shaped finials. The walls and pillars partly conceal the house from the road, and then reveal it gradually as the drive opens out into a courtyard. This is the south-facing facade of the house, in bright light for most of the day. The front door is in fact on the eastern side, where it is warmed by the morning sun. The previous owners built a stone terrace here, and we soon discovered it as the perfect spot for an early morning cup of tea. The only thing we miss at Fanshawe Gate is the last rays of the sunset, cut off by the hill above the house which reaches 900 feet at its highest point. As compensation, the garden is cut into the hill on various levels, and is naturally divided by walls or hedges into different areas, an ideal canvas for starting to create a garden.

When we arrived in the autumn of 1959, the driveway and many of the beds around the lawns were ablaze with huge show dahlias,

The lower courtyard and stackyard in 1944. Left: leading in the harvest. Middle: building corn ricks. Right: threshing corn sheaves.
Photographs from 'I Bought a Farm' by Roy Genders.

glowing red, orange, pink and white in the late, low sun. I felt quite overwhelmed by dahlias, and was happy to join the revolt against them in the next few years. Although it has taken forty years for the dahlia to be rehabilitated by fashionable gardeners, I suffered such a surfeit of dahlias the first time round that I am certainly not in the vanguard of the new movement. With the honourable exception of 'Bishop of Llandaff', for which I have always found a space, I will not plant another dahlia in the garden.

The recent revival of the dahlia has been unsettling, however. When we grubbed them up and threw them on the compost heap in the early 1960s, I was confident that we were replacing them with plants which were somehow better, more deserving, more sympathetic to their surroundings. For example, the driveway is now bordered by beds of roses, agapanthus, lavender and catmint, while clematis and climbing roses scramble up the stone walls. These plants seem to me to be the right ones in the right combination for this particular place. But I do sometimes ask myself: will any of our planting choices turn out to be as ephemeral as those 1950s dahlias? What determines fashions in gardening? Will a sharp-eyed garden historian spot some relics of the 1970s, some foibles and pretensions of the 1980s and 1990s? Probably. Does it matter? Almost certainly not.

I have been gardening for five decades and have seen several waves of fashion and changes in taste. My own knowledge has built up slowly, a gradual consolidation of snippets of horticultural know-how with experiments in design. The best thing about gardening is that it has been a shared life, since most of what I know, and many of my plants, have come from other people.

Dahlias, 1960.

The garden at Fanshawe Gate has emerged very gradually; slowly in the early years when all my energies went into bringing up the family, then more rapidly and radically as my domestic responsibilities grew less. These have been years of working hard to improve the soil, years of collecting cuttings and seeds, finding a place for gifts, and imagining constantly how a border might look in a few seasons' time.

I do not know whether to describe my love of gardening as a hobby, a way of life, or a passion. One thing is certain: it was never an option for me not to garden. I was brought up in a family where gardening was what you did whenever you stepped out of doors. I got off to an unpromising start in the eyes of my parents - although perhaps I was demonstrating that even the youngest children know what they like in a garden - when, aged just four, I knocked the heads off each tulip in my father's regimented border. I recently discovered a photograph from 1934, which must have been taken just before the demise of the tulips. That photograph, and the memory of the smacking I received, remind me why I still dislike the sight of tulips in municipally neat rows and am still tempted, though now a respectable pensioner, to decapitate one or two.

For my family, gardening standards were set by my grandfather. Grandfather Biggin lived and gardened in a grand, patriarchal style with obvious nostalgia for his Victorian youth. Aston Mount, his red brick-gabled, bay-windowed house in Dronfield stood on rising ground above formal terraces and rose pergolas. In spring, the borders were filled with ranks of wallflowers, tulips and polyanthus, followed in summer by geraniums (as we then called pelargoniums), yellow calceolaria, alyssum and lobelia. These bedding plants were grown in great quantities in Grandfather's glasshouses. There were six of these, heated by cast iron pipes connected to a boiler in a separate

Cynthia Ramsden (right) by her father's tulip border.

Grandfather Biggin's Dronfield garden in the early 1930s. The summer house is now at Fanshawe Gate.

building. A deep channel ran down the centre of each glasshouse. The channel was filled with water and covered with an ornamental iron grating which could be lifted to scoop up water in a zinc watering can. As a child, I lived in fear of the dark, still water, never really trusting to walk on the grates.

I also avoided the boiler house, where the immense boiler hissed away in the darkness. When Grandfather Biggin installed a hopper to feed coal to the beast more efficiently, it was a great event which the whole family was invited to watch. I remember standing well behind my parents, as close as possible to the door. Even more sinister than the boiler house was one particular small glasshouse which was hotter and steamier than the others. This was the fernery, filled with mysterious prehistoric fronds which I suspected could ensnare and slowly digest small girls, especially tulip murderers.

In contrast, real delight came from the other glasshouses, where abutilon, stephanotis and jasmine flourished in the year-round warmth. Grandfather grew pots of velvety gloxinias, and masses of spring flowers to bring into the house. From early February to late March the bay windows were filled with wonderfully scented plants. The display usually started with vast azaleas in tubs of oak and chrome, followed by daffodils, narcissi, tulips and hyacinth. The glasshouses also produced fruit: peaches, grapes, nectarines, lemons, and even melons. The melons were especially prized; they sat on the mahogany sideboard, wrapped in white napkins on a silver tray, and were forbidden to children. In the 1950s and 1960s, my Uncle Jack continued to grow lemons successfully in the same glasshouses. This was the beginning of the television age (we got ours for the Queen's coronation in 1952) and, while my grandfather's gardening achievements are recorded only in memory, Uncle Jack enjoyed a brief moment of media fame on television with Percy Thrower, demonstrating how to grow lemons in the northern climate.

Back to the 1930s. Every Saturday morning in summer, I used to walk up the hill to Aston Mount to collect a basket of vegetables for the weekend. There was a very strict rule: no vegetables would be handed over until I had returned the peapods from the previous week. For nothing was wasted in this garden; everything was returned to the earth through the vast compost and manure heaps. The vegetable garden itself was an

Grandfather Biggin in his garden.

27

Aerial view of Aston Mount, Dronfield.

impressive piece of land, stretching out for eighty yards behind the house. It bore little resemblance to our revived romantic notion of a gently ordered *potager;* this was a vegetable garden that meant business and was not going to be distracted by any unproductive decoration from its purpose of providing for three families. The rows of vegetables ran in absolutely straight lines, perfectly parallel or at right angles to each other. The plants grew in a solemn and upright fashion, tied up to canes or netted to thwart the birds, and the patterns of rotation and succession in the sowing were strictly observed. There was nothing dilettante about my grandfather's vegetable garden. The exotica were in the glasshouses, while the vegetable garden contained down to earth nourishment: potatoes, onions, carrots, peas, beans, turnips, cabbages, cauliflowers, sprouts, celery, asparagus, and rhubarb. The vegetables were women's work. The whole family ate dinner together on Sunday evening, and before going to church I would help my Aunt Bea to scrub a bucketful of potatoes, or to pod peas and broad beans gathered in a cane washing basket. Aunt Bea dealt with her muddy hands by tipping neat Domestos bleach on them, rinsing them under the tap, and then splashing on some Chanel No.5. Sitting next to her in church, I dreaded the moment when the smell of Domestos finally overpowered the Chanel No.5.

Not surprisingly, Grandfather Biggin employed a full-time gardener to keep the cycle of propagating, bedding, lifting, digging, rotting and replenishing going in all its steaming glory. I was expected to help too, and I was paid a penny a bucket for picking stones, and a halfpenny a bucket for dandelions. I was a willing helper, for this was decent pocket money in the 1930s. When I tried a similar scheme with my own children at Fanshawe Gate, they were quick to point out that I should index the original penny for inflation since the 1930s. When we had done a rough calculation it suddenly seemed, from my point of view, to be rather expensive labour. I realised, as do many gardeners, that there is no cheap and easy way out of the hard work.

David Noble, 1969.

29

Fanshawe Gate Hall as a working farm in the early 1900s.

2 derbyshire stone

The garden at Fanshawe Gate has been given a strong structure by the natural materials of the house and its surroundings. The mellow Derbyshire gritstone and sandstone of the 16th century Hall are repeated in the imposing stone gateposts and dovecote, relics of a once larger house, and in the walls which divide and surround the gardens.

If we had never planted a thing at Fanshawe Gate, the garden would still have been a place of great beauty. The garden is a series of terraces, cut into the lower slopes of the Pennines as they begin to rise to the Derbyshire Peak District. Each level is supported by massive drystone walls, some rising to 15 feet, built of the same mellow mixture of gritstone and sandstone as the house, dovecote and gateposts. We could not have wished for a more versatile backdrop for planting. Steely grey under a low Pennine sky, Derbyshire stone is transformed by summer or winter sun. The south-facing walls reflect the sun intensely from beneath their summer covering of roses and clematis. Even when bare in winter, the stone still glows warmly against frost or snow. The north-facing walls are quite different; they do not even look as if they are built of the same material, with their soft green moss, sheltering ferns and shade-loving plants.

Stone has created the backbone of the garden and provided inspiration for our planting. Its texture is delightfully varied. In some places it is trimmed and dressed, as in the mullions and quoins of the house and dovecote, or in the finials which top the high gateposts at either end of the entrance driveway. Elsewhere it is rough and uneven, but still placed in skilful regularity to form the drystone walls which flank the driveway, divide the different levels, and border the whole property.

We have found some interesting stone artefacts and containers in the garden, many of them reflecting the industrial and farming traditions of the region. Lying around the garden are several millstones, which we discovered piled up as a pillar supporting doors in an old outbuilding. They are now planted with hostas and alpines, and are satisfyingly difficult for slugs and snails to climb. Then there are the mushroom-shaped staddle stones, which stand half hidden under trees in the shadiest part of the garden. With their giant stone beams, they look like a sort of domestic Stonehenge. They were in fact used to support hay and corn, and to protect the crops from rats and mice. As far as I have been able to find out, the word 'staddle' seems to be derived from the Old English 'stathol', meaning a base, and may be related to the Old Norse 'stothull' (a cow pen). There is also an Old High German word 'stadal', meaning a barn. In fact, barns are supported on staddles in some areas, although I don't think I have seen any in Derbyshire. We have risked vertebrae and toes transporting these megaliths to better positions within the garden, but they very quickly settle down and moss over. Now they look as if they have grown from the soil, a few inches every hundred years.

The stone dovecote was restored in 1991.

Staddle stones in the Elizabethan garden.

Spring planting in a stone trough.

The stone mounting block before its removal to the stackyard.

We were lucky to discover such treasures in the garden, and even luckier with stone pieces found elsewhere. We have always hoarded materials unwanted and discarded by others, even though bringing them home has not been easy. Kind farming neighbours have often helped out with blocks and tackle, rollers and low-loaders to collect our finds. These include the solid stone mounting block from my grandmother's childhood home, a farm now swallowed by the Sheffield suburb of Greenhill. We also have an enormous stone trough from Holt House in Matlock, where I worked as the WRVS Organiser for the Derbyshire Dales.

We have found materials in unlikely places. Years ago, when Sheffield Corporation was digging up old pavements, John negotiated to buy enough stone paving to create a new terrace at Fanshawe Gate. These old flagstones have transplanted easily into their new rural setting. One of them does contain a reference to its urban past, and I wonder whether any of our visitors have ever spotted it: the face of a small boy carved into the stone. I wonder who he was, and when the carving was made. Whether it was done at the end of the 19th century or in the early part of the 20th century, I suppose that the scene would have been the same: I imagine a boy sitting on the front step of his terraced house in Sheffield, perhaps near one of the steelworks, with the paved and cobbled street as his only playground, and a pocket knife as his only toy. The carving would have taken him some time, so I have always discounted the possibility that it might have been the work of a later, spray-paint generation.

The stone has given us an excellent framework for the garden, but it is one we have struggled to maintain. In our first years at Fanshawe Gate, we were often woken in the night by an echoing rumble, which we came to dread, knowing that the morning light would reveal a mound of stone and wet earth somewhere in the garden. I don't know why the walls generally gave way in the night. The orchard wall did once collapse on a sunny day, when our oldest cat was snoozing beneath it. I assumed he was lost, but his sixth sense must have given him a moment's warning, for he reappeared some time later when he had got over the shock. So perhaps the night-time collapses reduced the possible casualties. The huge wall which supports the vegetable garden 12 feet above the courtyard collapsed for the first time in the mid-1960s. It was soon followed by the even taller stackyard wall, which separates the old tithe barn and stables from the main part of the garden, and by one of the walls along the main driveway. In each case, the pressure of damp earth and seeping water proved too strong, and we have had to learn to incorporate drainage as we painstakingly rebuild each wall.

The greatest threat to our walls nowadays comes from Russian vine, *Fallopia baldschuanica* syn. *Polygonum baldschuanicum*. I'm glad to say that we are not responsible for planting it; the Russian vine was there with the show dahlias back in 1959. Unlike the dahlias, it is impossible to get rid of, no matter how feverishly hard we try. There are few plants I loathe, but this is one of them, and I apologise if you love its frothy white flowers or its virtue of speedily smothering everything in its neighbourhood. We should not blame it too bitterly; it is undoubtedly a victim of ignorance of its need for wide open spaces. Gardening books, of course, used to recommend it for disguising 'unsightly objects'. In my view you would have to be cursed with an unusually unsightly power station at the bottom of your garden to risk planting it. Also known as the Mile-a-minute plant, Russian vine has an extraordinary ability to rise from the dead. We have tried everything: digging it up, chopping it out, burning it and poisoning it. Our triumph rarely lasts for more than a week before an invisible sliver buried deep inside the wall suddenly appears as a three-foot frond, waving cheerfully as it emerges from the stonework. Undoubtedly it will still be there to welcome the return of the dahlia, if some future gardener is so inclined.

Staddle stones in the shade.

The stone trough from Holt House, Matlock.

The Russian vine apart, I still feel that the walled entrance driveway is one of the best examples of how well the Derbyshire stone sets off plants. The walls run for some 80 feet, drawing the eye towards the south face of the house. The beginning and end of each wall is punctuated by the 15-foot high stone gateposts, relics of the house in its more important days. At the foot of the walls, deep beds have given us the space to create a strong and atmospheric entrance, using colour and rhythm in the planting.

We have changed the look of the driveway several times. In 1960 we replaced the dahlias with roses: 'Golden Showers' against the walls and hybrid tea roses in mixed colours at the front of the border. For many years, my grandfather's influence still strong, we continued to plant out summer bedding - pelargoniums, alyssum and lobelia - along the drive. Looking back, I was surprisingly disciplined about the bedding plants. Just before the birth of my second son in June 1964, I was so large that I could hardly see the ground at my feet, let alone bend down with a trowel, yet I still managed to complete the summer planting before setting off for the hospital.

'Golden Showers' roses are notoriously vulnerable to black spot, but we like them so much on the walls of the driveway that we have simply replaced the original roses with new stock whenever necessary. We picked up a good idea from Sir Reresby Sitwell, the owner

Aerial view of Fanshawe Gate Hall from the east.

of Renishaw Hall, whose gardens we have long admired. He suggested that we could plant pink 'Sexy Rexy' roses at the entrance to the gates. Interplanted with soft blue *Nepeta racemosa* syn. *N. mussinii*, these create a classic English garden look. The feel of this planting is altogether softer than the marigolds which it replaced. Marigolds, like dahlias, have also endured several years of disapproval, although before we could remove ours they were picked by a passing group of chanting, saffron-robed Hare Krishna followers. They wove the marigolds into garlands and left them at the gates for us, so we moved away from that period of garden fashion complete with the monks' blessing.

We have kept the approaches to the garden fairly traditional, but I became keen to experiment with different planting within the gates, especially as the children grew up and I began to have more time. Before changing the driveway yet again, however, we put into practice a lesson we had learned over the years: that the soil must be well prepared. Much of the beauty of a garden comes from the health and vitality of well chosen plants growing in conditions which suit them. The beds along the drive had poor soil which was difficult to dig, and the plants we liked would not thrive there. We worked the soil for days, digging it over and forking in large quantities of manure which we removed from a neighbouring field with a borrowed digger. The result showed immediately in vibrant, vigorous plants. Had we known

Standard 'Happy Child' roses now line the driveway, while Nepeta racemosa forms substantial mounds at the front of the borders. The walls support various clematis in shades of blue: C.viticella 'Purpurea Plena Elegans'; C.alpina 'Frances Rivis', and C.'Lady Betty Balfour' (the latter has yellow stamens). These are mixed with the yellow C.orientalis (the 'orange peel' clematis).

what an extraordinarily transforming effect this soil preparation would have, we would have perhaps done it earlier, and spared ourselves several years of disappointments. Now we go through this same procedure whenever we remake or refresh a bed. While the digging is necessary to bring about a quick improvement in neglected soil, it should not be repeated too often. As I explain in Chapter 6, we damaged the soil structure in some of the beds through over-enthusiastic double digging. On the other hand, a strict annual routine of spreading manure does make a significant difference to the quality of the plants.

I decided to be bold with the current planting along the drive. I wanted to move away from soft pastel shades, and to work out a scheme in dramatic colours, such as blue and gold. Inspiration for the planting came from Nada Jennett, whom I met at the English Gardening School where she lectures. She pointed out how a line of standard roses planted down each side of the drive would reinforce the lines drawing the eye towards the house. We planted standards of golden 'Happy Child' roses from David Austin, and echoed their mop heads with blue *Agapanthus* 'Headbourne Hybrids' between each rose. 'Munstead' lavender brings smudges of powdery blue to the back of the border. At the front of the border *Nepeta racemosa* syn. *N. mussinii* and *Alchemilla mollis* mingle in a blend of blue and gold. Alchemilla, of course, is a terrible self-seeder and spreads itself everywhere. But, unlike Russian vine, alchemilla's charm compels me to forgive it.

Gill Buck, 1998.

3 water

There is plenty of water in this part of the Pennines, and water looks beautiful against Derbyshire stone. The old farmyard pond at Fanshawe Gate has been restored, and running water introduced through two new water features: a stone waterfall, and a controversial cherub, known as the Pissing Nymph.

Water associates well with Derbyshire stone. It is certainly a familiar combination to our eyes in this damp corner of the Pennines.

Water is a delight in the garden, but for many years we had little more than a few stone troughs. As these were shared between dogs, cats, birds and children, they were mostly muddy puddles of greenish slime. We scrubbed them out occasionally with Jeyes Fluid, and dreamed about the limpid pools and crystal waterfalls we would have preferred.

As the children grew older, we could see that our eldest son, Mark, had inherited my grandfather's enthusiasm for garden projects on a grand scale. Anything that involved mechanics, construction, or the shifting of vast quantities of earth fascinated him. When the boys were in their teens, we gave them a second-hand dumper truck. They loved driving it around, and were very happy to use their toy to help with major works in the garden. Mark was also good at improvising, and so with only limited resources we were able to venture into the world of water features without once resorting to a garden centre.

Controversy still rumbles around my first water project, the Pissing Nymph. The name has stuck, although I hope that its opponents who first christened it now use the name with as much affection as malice. Opinions on this little cherub in an old stone trough divide as follows. Against: professional gardeners, horticulturalists, teachers of garden design, and art historians. For: me, and the majority of visitors on open days, who race each other to sit on the wooden bench within the sound of the cherub's trickling water. The cherub may be kitsch, but all around his trough is a marvellous sense of peace. Overhanging him is a small *Salix matsudana* 'Tortuosa'. This plant is the survivor of a bouquet of flowers given to my daughter-in-law, Ruth, when her first child was born. Living in a gentrifying part of London, the bouquet naturally included some designer twigs. Left in the vase for weeks while Ruth coped with the new baby, the designer twigs produced roots. I potted some up for Ruth, and some for myself. Planted behind the cherub, the Salix always reminds me of my first grandson.

The paving around the cherub's trough supports a mixture of permanent and seasonal planting. *Phormium tenax* 'Bronze Baby' provides a consistent architectural form. The spring planting is bright and sunny: snowdrops, species *Crocus* 'Advance'

The Pissing Nymph, with Phormium tenax 'Bronze Baby'.

Stackyard trough with Marsh marigolds.

47

and 'Snowbunting', *Iris reticulata* 'Harmony', miniature *Narcissus* 'Golden Bells' with their yellow hooped skirts, and *Puschkinia scilloides libanotica*. *Iris pseudacorus* follows in summer, with various thymes, miniature pinks, *Sedum spathulifolium*, and *Helianthemum lunulatum*.

I feel that the Pissing Nymph has become part of our landscape, and I am now more or less deaf to high-flown criticisms of it. I also get a great deal of pleasure from knowing how it was made. As I have said before, Mark is good at improvisation, and is also a natural hoarder of materials which 'might come in useful one day' as he puts it. As a mother, his messy collecting infuriated me, but as a gardener I have come to appreciate it. Heaven knows why he was keeping an old lavatory cistern, but it is now there holding a small pump, buried in the ground beneath the cherub's trough. In high summer I top up the cistern with a watering can every two or three days. As I can't actually see it, I pour until I can see water bubbling up through the stone paving, then I run round to the log store to switch on the pump.

The next project was more ambitious. I doubt that we would have embarked on building a 12-foot waterfall above the courtyard without Mark's infectious enthusiasm and readiness to take on the work. We set ourselves the deadline of completing it in time for our youngest daughter Anna's wedding in July 1994. Having organised weddings for the two older girls, we already knew the dangers. Such events are the catalyst for spring cleaning the house, then completely redecorating it, then pulling down the east wing and rebuilding it, until only

Astilbe 'Venus'.

Preparing and planting the pond below the waterfall.

48

the dawning of the wedding day puts a stop to the spiral of improvement. So we should have known better. At the same time, without the pressure of a looming deadline, many projects would never get off the ground. Mark's adrenalin carried him through all the construction of stone ledges up the height of the wall, and the fixing of a lion's head through which the waterfall would begin. But on the wedding day, the pump was still not installed.

We were saved from disappointment by our neighbour, Robert Boden. With all the down to earth ingenuity of a Derbyshire farmer, he fixed a hosepipe to a tap, ran it through the orchard above the courtyard, and shoved it through the lion's mouth. It worked perfectly, and the wedding guests enjoyed the gentle splash of water throughout the reception. I, however, kept a nervous watch on the ground beneath our feet. I knew that the project had also stopped short of a pool liner, so the water was simply draining through the earth and gathering underneath the marquee.

We got away with it. The wedding celebrations stayed on firm ground, and a few days later the waterfall was connected up to its pump. We built a stone terrace in front of the pool, which has made a wonderful place to sit, filled with the scent of nearby roses, and calmed by the soft greens of the surrounding planting. Water splashes off the stone ledges and on to rocks below, which are surrounded by moisture-loving plants. These include *Hosta* 'August Moon', *H.* 'Blue Lake', *H. fortunei* 'Aureomarginata', and *H.* 'Wide Brim'. We have *Iris ensata*, *I. pseudacorus* 'Variegata', *I. pallida* 'Variegata', and *I. sibirica*. There are two varieties of astilbe: *A.* 'White Diamond' and *A.* 'Deutschland'. Other plants include *Symphytum* 'Goldsmith', *Rodgersia pinnata* 'Elegans', *Crocosmia* 'Lucifer', the candelabra *Primula bulleyana*, *Persicaria virginiana* 'Painter's Palette', and the black *Ophiopogon planiscapus* 'Nigrescens'. Against the walls on either side of the waterfall we have trained *Cornus alba* 'Elegantissima' and *Cornus alba* 'Spaethii', mingled with *Sambucus racemosa* 'Sutherland Gold'.

Our biggest mistake in the waterfall planting was to give room to the variegated ground elder, *Aegopodium podagraria* 'Variegatum'. As far as I am concerned, this invasive plant is the new Russian vine. I think that the dangers of ground elder are more widely known now than when we planted it in 1994, but it took us some time to appreciate its full horror. It performed soberly enough in the woodland areas of the

Damaged ash tree and timber ready for turning.

BTCV volunteers dig out the old pond.

garden, lighting up dark corners and not advancing too swiftly. However, in the sunny, moist conditions of the waterfall it soon spread rampantly through the other plants. Ground elder is astonishingly difficult to dig out, but we realised that if we did not do it quickly, the whole border would soon be invaded. After much painful and tedious digging, we extricated the waterfall planting from its grip. That, I am sorry to say, was not the end of our battle with ground elder: this particular garden thug will reappear in later chapters.

Our most recent water project is the restoration of the old farm pond in the stackyard below the house. It is a beautiful pond, which waters the roots of an enormous, very old ash tree. The stackyard and its barn were in fact under separate ownership from the main house for many years. It is only since we bought the barn in 1998 that we have been able to restore the area around it, exposing its old paved threshold and making a home for our ducks and hens.

Four years ago we feared that we were about to lose the ash tree. An arboriculturalist who ring-dated it calculated that it was over 400 years old. It had lost its vigour, and one of the main branches fell during a gale, bringing down three more branches with it. A few days later we heard the tree groaning. We ran to move a car parked beneath it, getting clear of the tree just before the longest remaining branch crashed across the pond and the stackyard. We could see that other branches were vulnerable, so we called in tree surgeons in the hope that the rest of the tree could be saved. It has survived, losing some of its majesty and grace, but happily reinvigorated. The fallen branches were spotted by a visitor, Jim Brown, who asked if he could take some of the wood, still in its green state, for turning. A week later, he and his wife Eileen brought us two beautiful little bowls. They were almost transparent, with a satin-like surface, and edged in bark. Jim has since made bowls and candlesticks from the remainder of the wood. All the children now have a piece, to remind them of the tree where they used to climb and make dens. Jim continues to produce pieces from the old ash tree, which he sells for a charity, PACT (Parents' Association for Children with Tumours). He sometimes has a stall in the garden on open days.

The pond beneath the ash tree was restored as our millennium project by the British Trust for Conservation Volunteers (BTCV). A group of them bravely camped in the barn for a week and spent their days digging and puddling clay into the base of the pond.

water

The ducks were suspicious at first, but are now completely at home on the pond. However, building ponds is an old art, and we have not got ours quite right. The water has remained stubbornly cloudy, dashing our hopes that it would clear after a few months. This may turn out to be one of those projects that must be painfully repeated until we have built up the necessary experience.

The spring display of daffodils on the banks of the pond is one of the best in the garden. Many of the bulbs come from our old friends John and Julia Taylor, the well-known growers in Holbeach, who send us a large carton of bulbs from their farm every autumn. I enjoy opening up the packs and anticipating spring in the array of glossy illustrations. Planting the bulbs is backbreaking, and I am usually so relieved to finish that I forget to make a note of what I have planted and where. I also forget to note where the bulbs were once the flowers have died down. When the Taylor's bulbs arrive the next autumn, I can never be quite sure what I am planting them next to. I just plunge them into the soil and hope for the best.

B. Franklin, 1990.

spring

4 new ideas for old borders

In the last few years, two borders have been completely redesigned to suit their orientation. A rockery and heather border has been replaced with hostas and ferns, while the Elizabethan garden has become home to an unusual experiment in massed variegated planting. The latter was recently rescued from near - destruction by variegated ground elder.

The north-facing courtyard border, replanted with ferns and hostas.

You can never tell with gardens when a new source of inspiration will appear. It could be a book, a magazine, a television programme or a friend's garden. The most significant recent influence on the garden at Fanshawe Gate came in the unexpected form of a sword dancer.

While morris dancing is very well known in Derbyshire, sword dancing is more unusual. Rather than the white trousers, handkerchiefs and bells of the morris dancers, sword dancers wear the early 19th century uniform of the Hussars. The origins of this are said to be that a militia troop passed on their uniforms to some local men, who then formed a team of sword dancers. Anna, my youngest daughter, invited the Handsworth Sword Dancers to dance at her wedding. This, of course, was the day when I could think of little else than the marsh being created by our improvised waterfall, so I only had half an eye on the dancers. I was still distracted when one of them gave me his card. I put it away in a safe place, which usually means, in our house, that it is never seen again. By great fortune, the card reappeared a few days later.

The variegated border in the Elizabethan garden.

The Handsworth Sword Dancers at Haddon Hall: John Pitts is second from the right. Photograph by Mary Lester.

57

Top: Meconopsis cambrica 'Muriel Brown'.
Bottom: Polystichum setiferum.

When the wedding celebration was over, we had to get down to some hard work. We had put to the back of our minds the fact that, only the following weekend, we were due to open the garden for the first time to raise money for the Derbyshire Wildlife Trust. We were quite unprepared, and we knew that the cosmetic tidying for the wedding (only the bits the guests would see) would not be good enough for an open day. I became desperate as time raced on, and then I found the sword dancer's card. He was called John Pitts, and his name was followed by the magic words 'gardener and horticulturalist'. I crossed my fingers and called his number.

As soon as John Pitts arrived, we could see that his energy and enthusiasm extended far beyond sword dancing. His knowledge of plants is profound, and he had already done much research into plant history. Soon we were all caught up in the endless possibilities for the garden, inspired by John's knowledge and ideas. He sorted us out for that rushed open day, and then returned to tackle other parts of the garden which had caught his eye.

Two borders in particular were completely redesigned and replanted with John's help: the north-facing bed in the courtyard, and the east-facing bed in the walled Elizabethan garden.

The north-facing courtyard bed had become rather damp and sour. We had a rockery there, at the time when they were fashionable, and we also grew heathers. There was an espaliered morello cherry against the wall, but it all looked rather dull. With John's encouragement, we took out everything. We replaced all the soil in the bed, bringing in tractor loads of new soil and manure; heavy work, but at least the materials are readily available out in the country. The new bed, based on ferns and hostas with splashes of colour from poppies, remains fresh and interesting from spring through to autumn.

John chose carefully for colour, form and texture. Some of the ferns were unfamiliar to us: amongst them are *Asplenium scolopendrium* 'Crispum', *Matteuccia, Polystichum setiferum, Dryopteris*, and my favourite, the delicate *Athyrium filix-femina* 'Frizelliae'. The hostas include *H.* 'Thomas Hogg', *H. fortunei* 'Albopicta', *H.* 'Honeybells', *H.* 'Frances Williams', *H. sieboldiana* var. *elegans, H.* 'August Moon', and *H. fortunei* 'Aureomarginata'. The poppy 'Muriel Brown' has self seeded in the bed, and we also

Top: The variegated border in the Elizabethan garden. Bottom: The fern and hosta border in the upper courtyard.

have *Meconopsis betonicifolia*, the blue Himalayan poppy. There are *Primula vialii*, short-lived but very attractive, and blue *Teucrium fruticans* at the front edge. The ivy *Hedera helix* 'Goldheart' glows from the wall behind. A pink foxglove has established itself between the stones of the wall. Although we had not planned to have any pink in this bed, it is too pretty to take out.

The variegated border in the Elizabethan garden was quite an experiment for us. John Pitts gave us the courage to make some unusual plant and colour combinations, and the effect is obviously novel for many people, because this is where the most lively discussions take place on open days. I used to think that variegated plants should not be massed together, but planted individually as a statement or focal point. John turned that idea on its head in the most extraordinary way. He chose plants for their height, leaf form and structure, and then reduced the dissonance of their variegation by planting, at intervals, blocks of striking bronze-coloured plants.

Altogether, there are over 100 different species in this border, which is 30 feet wide and 6 feet deep.

The shrubs include *Solanum dulcamara* 'Variegatum', *Philadelphus* 'Innocence', *Photinia davidiana* 'Palette', *Prunus laurocerasus* 'Castlewellan', *Deutzia scabra* 'Variegata', *Escallonia* 'Silver Anniversary', *Weigela florida* 'Variegata', *Cornus controversa* 'Variegatus', *Sambucus nigra* 'Madonna' and the variegated form of *Forsythia x intermedia* 'Spectabilis'. The bronze plantings include *Lysimachia ciliata* 'Firecracker', *Foeniculum vulgare* 'Purpureum', *Dahlia* 'Bishop of Llandaff', *Canna* 'Black Knight' (the two latter are planted as annuals) and, at the front of the border, *Ajuga reptans* 'Burgundy Glow', *Heuchera macrantha* 'Palace Purple' and *Viola riviniana* 'Purpurea'.

When this border was planted in 1995, the presence of several clumps of ground elder, *Aegopodium podagraria* 'Variegatum', went unnoticed amid all the variegation. Only in 2000, after we had saved the waterfall border from this evilly invasive plant, did we realise that it had also spread throughout the variegated border. By then, it was too late. In the spring of 2001 we had the backbreaking, heartbreaking task of taking out every plant in the variegated border. For several days we dug, lifted, sieved soil from roots and tried to tease out the long white thread-like roots of the ground elder. If we

Primula vialii.

Dahlia 'Bishop of Llandaff'.

thought we could save a plant, we washed its roots under the tap and potted it up ready for replanting. But almost three quarters of the original herbaceous planting was lost, inextricably choked up by the ground elder. We have now replaced most of the lost plants in order to restore the border to the scheme shown in the following diagram. As I contemplate the cost, in time and money, my hatred of variegated ground elder is confirmed. We should have known that this plant must only be used in dry and shaded areas where not much else grows – the RHS Encyclopedia is quite clear on this point – and it was a terrible mistake to plant it in sunny and moist conditions. It now shocks me to see *A. podagraria* 'Variegatum' on sale in garden centres. I could have given away mounds of the stuff free; except of course that I would never do that now, not even to my worst enemy. You will not find it for sale at our open days.

David Noble, 1969.

variegated border

1 Hosta undulata 'Albomarginata' (Plantain lily)
2 Pachysandra terminalis 'Variegata'
3 Fuchsia magellanica 'Variegata'
4 Leucothoe fontanesiana 'Rainbow' (Switch Ivy)
5 Cornus controversa 'Variegata' (Dogwood)
6 Nicotiana langsdorffii 'Cream Splash' (Tobacco plant)
7 Geranium phaeum 'Variegatum' (Cranesbill)
8 Symphytum x uplandicum 'Variegatum' (Comfrey)
9 Osmanthus heterophyllus 'Variegatus'
10 Viburnum tinus 'Variegatum'
11 Olearia traversii 'Variegata' (Daisy bush)
12 Ajuga reptans 'Rainbow' (Bugle)
13 Symphytum 'Goldsmith'
14 Phlox paniculata 'Harlequin'
15 Fuchsia 'Tom West'
16 Salvia officinalis 'Icterina' (Common sage)
17 Lysimachia ciliata 'Firecracker' (Loosestrife)
18 Melissa officinalis 'Aurea' (Lemon balm)
19 Symphoricarpos orbiculatus 'Foliis Variegatis' (Coral berry)
20 Forsythia x intermedia 'Spectabilis'
21 Humulus lupulus 'Aureus' (Hop)
22 Saponaria officinalis 'Dazzler' (Soapwort)
23 Ajuga reptans 'Variegata'
24 Geranium macrorrhizum 'Variegatum'
25 Mentha x piperita f.citrata (Lemon mint)

26 Physostegia virginiana 'Variegata' (Obedient plant)
27 Sambucus nigra 'Madonna' (Black elder)
28 Phalaris arundinacea var. picta (Gardeners' garters)
29 Veronica gentianoides 'Variegata' (Speedwell)
30 Plantago lanceolata 'Streaker'
31 Houttuynia cordata 'Chameleon'
32 Aquilegia vulgaris 'Woodside' (Columbine)
33 Lysimachia punctata 'Alexander'
34 Rubus microphyllus 'Variegatus'
35 Weigela florida 'Variegata'
36 Jasminum officinale f. affine 'Argenteovariegatum'
37 Amoracia rusticana 'Variegata'
38 Kerria japonica 'Picta' (Jew's mantle)
39 Myosotis scorpioides 'Blaqua' (Forget-me-not)
40 Heuchera micrantha 'Palace Purple'
41 Polemonium caeruleum 'Blanjou' (Jacob's ladder)
42 Jasminum officinale f. affine 'Aureum'
43 Tanacetum vulgare 'Silver Lace' (Tansy)
44 Artemisia lactiflora 'Guizhou' (Mugwort)

45 Rhamnus alaternus 'Argenteo variegata'
46 Silene dioica 'Graham's Delight' (Campion)
47 Ophiopogon planiscapus 'Nigrescens', (Lilyturf)
48 Phlox paniculata 'Harlequin'
49 Cimicifuga racemosa 'Brunette' (Bugbane)
50 Cornus alba 'Elegantissima'
51 Acer negundo 'Elegans' (Ash-leaved maple)
52 Sambucus nigra 'Guincho Purple'
53 Miscanthus sinensis 'Zebrinus' (Zebra grass)
54 Solidago flexicaulis 'Variegatus' (Golden rod)
55 Clematis recta 'Purpurea'
56 Sambucus nigra 'Albomarginata'
57 Astrantia major 'Sunningdale Variegated'
58 Heuchera 'Snowstorm'
59 Mentha x gracilis 'Variegata' (Gingermint)
60 Cornus coronarius 'Variegatus'
61 Silybum marianum (Blessed Mary's thistle)
62 Trifolium pratense 'Susan Smith' (Clover)

63 Eleutherococcus sieboldianus 'Variegatus'
64 Solanum dulcamara 'Variegatum'
65 Brunnera macrophylla 'Dawson's White'
66 Ilex x altaclerensis 'Lawsoniana' (Holly)
67 Lamium maculatum f. album 'Friday'
   (Dead nettle)
68 Sambucus racemosa 'Sutherland Gold'
69 Scrophularia auriculata 'Burdung'
   (Figwort)
70 Plantago major 'Purpurea' (Plantain)
71 Philadelphus 'Innocence' (Mock orange)
72 Duchesnea indica 'Harlequin'
73 Oenanthe javanica 'Flamingo'
74 Syringa vulgaris 'Variegated Double'
   (Lilac)
75 Photinia davidiana 'Palette'
76 Barbarea vulgaris 'Variegata'
   (St. Barbara's herb)
77 Pulmonaria 'David Ward' (Lungwort)
78 Brunnera macrophylla 'Hadspen Cream'
79 Prunus laurocerasus 'Castlewellan'
   (Ornamental cherry)
80 Geranium x monacense 'Variegatum'
81 Iris pseudacorus 'Variegata'
82 Persicaria virginiana 'Painter's Palette'

83 Ceanothus 'Zanzibar' (California lilac)
84 Pyracantha coccinea 'Harlequin'
   (Firethorn)
85 Lavatera arborea 'Variegata' (Mallow)
86 Berberis thunbergii 'Rose Glow' (Barbary)
87 Buddleja davidii 'Harlequin'
88 Deutzia scabra 'Variegata'
89 Escallonia 'Silver Anniversary'
90 Corylus maxima 'Red Filbert' (Hazel)
91 Hydrangea petiolaris
92 Symphoricarpos orbiculatus
   'Taff's Silver Edge' (Snowberry)
93 Sedum spurium 'Variegatum' (Stonecrop)
94 Foeniculum vulgare 'Purpureum' (Fennel)
95 Berberis thunbergii 'Atropurpureum'
96 Forsythia 'Fiesta'
97 Weigela florida 'Foliis Purpureis'
98 Ficus carica 'Brown Turkey' (Fig)
99 Cotoneaster horizontalis 'Variegata'
100 Polygonatum x striatum
   'Variegatum' (Solomons seal)
101 Cortaderia selloana 'Aureolineata'
   (Pampas grass)

5 historical planting

The buildings at Fanshawe Gate date from the 16th century. There are many references to the history of the house and the Fanshawe family in the ornamentation of the garden, particularly the wrought iron weather vane and gates. Some borders have been redesigned to include plants which would have been known in the 16th century, while traditional fruit and nut trees – walnut, medlar, mulberry and fig – are being planted for each grandchild. Topiary in many shapes and sizes brings the garden to life in winter.

winter

Although Fanshawe Gate dates back to the 13th century, the architecture of the present house is predominantly 16th century. We have tried to incorporate references to this period in the ornamentation of the garden. In 1979, the quatercentenary of the founding of Henry Fanshawe's school in Dronfield, we commissioned a weather vane based on the pennon of Henry Fanshawe. This sits on the roof of the Cottage, a separate building which was once part of the original, larger house.

More recently, to mark our Ruby wedding anniversary, John and I designed a pair of wrought iron gates to replace the wooden five-bar gate at the entrance to the house. These gates also incorporate a Fanshawe coat of arms. It was one thing to design the gates on paper, but quite another to find somebody to make them since they measure ten feet wide by eight feet high and weigh a good half-ton. We tentatively approached Steve Jackson, a blacksmith whose business my daughter Louise helped to set up through the Sheffield Enterprise Agency. Steve had made some wrought iron lights for us, and was very enthusiastic to tackle the gates, his largest project so far. Unfortunately he dropped a half-completed gate on his foot. He managed to hobble around with his broken foot in plaster, and found the patience to supervise Mark, who was brought in as an emergency helper to finish the work.

We had thought rather less about the history of planting until we got to know John Pitts. John's research gave us information on plants which were known in England in the 16th and 17th centuries, and we have included many of these, either the species or cultivars, in beds around the house and the lawn.

The east-facing borders which flank the front door to the house contain our most extensive collection of historic plants. In the planting list overleaf I have given the common names of many of them. Even the names alone - Mugwort, Goatsbeard, Traveller's Joy - give a feel of the distant past.

The weather vane incorporating the pennon - the knight's flag - of Henry Fanshawe.

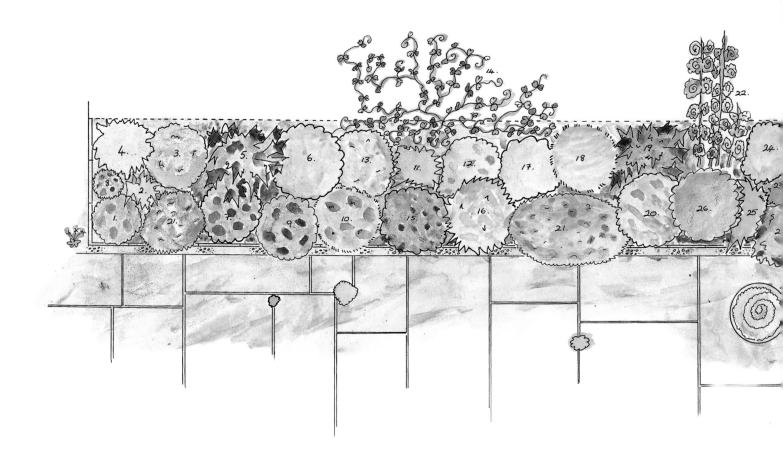

hall borders

Old Hall

27 Nepeta mussinii
28 Geum 'Georgenberg'
29 Alcea rosea 'Chater's Double Pink'
30 Geranium x oxonianum 'Stillingfleet'
31 Origanum vulgare 'Aureum' (Wild
   marjoram)
32 Lavatera trimestris 'Pink Cup' (Mallow)
33 Penstemon 'Garnet'
34 Geranium dalmaticum
35 Lathyrus 'White Pearl' (Everlasting pea)

36 Thalictrum cultratum
37 Salvia cacaliifolia
38 Geum rivale 'Lionel Cox'
39 Aruncus dioicus 'Kneiffii' (Goatsbeard)
40 Phlox maculata 'Natascha'
41 Amsonia orientalis
42 X Pardancanda norrisii
43 Astrantia major (Masterwort)
44 Potentilla 'William Rollison' (Cinquefoil)
45 Polemonium caeruleum (Jacob's ladder)

46 Symphyandra pendula
47 Lunaria annua 'Alba Variegata'
   (Honesty)
48 Buxus sempervirens (Box)

Illustration not to scale

71

These beds looked very different in our early years at Fanshawe Gate. In keeping with the fashion of the times and my own gardening inheritance, they were planted out each year with antirrhinum, alyssum and trailing lobelia. In spring they were packed with tulips and wallflowers. We love the new beds, but we do miss the wallflowers, whose evocative perfume reminds my husband John of childhood Easters at Skegness. Last year we revisited Skegness, and John went on his own quiet pilgrimage to the municipal flower beds. He was overcome with delight to find them still bursting with wallflowers, just as they were over sixty years ago.

John Pitts helped us to transform two difficult beds which face north, running from the dovecote along one end of the lawn, and backed by the stone wall which separates the Elizabethan garden from the main garden. The soil in this dovecote lawn border was always damp and sour, and tended to spill down onto the grass. We only ever managed to grow a few junipers there. Before replanting, we completely reconstructed the beds to deepen and contain them. Mark came up with the idea of placing stone setts as an edging, and fixing stone roofing slates on end inside them to retain the soil. As with our other new beds, we completely rejuvenated the soil with lots of manure. Now, although these beds only measure two feet from front to back, they support some rich planting. The climbing roses 'Lord Byron', 'Danse du Feu' and 'Gloire de Dijon' seem to thrive against the stone wall, and support other climbers such as climbing nasturtium, *Tropaeolum tuberosum* var. *lineamaculatum* 'Ken Aslet', and *Jasminum beesianum*. There is also a honeysuckle from the house of a much-loved aunt and uncle. They planted the honeysuckle only shortly before they both died, and we could not bear to leave it when their house was sold.

Many of the historic plants from the Hall borders are repeated in the dovecote lawn border.

Wallflowers in the Hall border before its redesign.

Junipers in the dovecote lawn border before its redesign.

summer

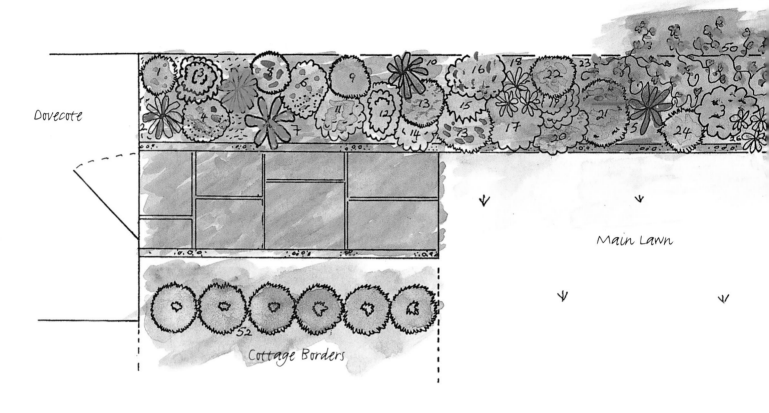

Elizabethan Garden

Dovecote

Main Lawn

Cottage Borders

dovecote lawn border

1 Kitaibela vitifolia
2 Geranium x monacense 'Muldoon' (Cranesbill)
3 Campanula 'E K Toogood' (Bellflower)
4 Salvia fargesii
5 Geranium x oxonianum 'Sherwood'
6 Campanula pyramidalis 'Alba'
7 Geranium macrorrhizum
8 Boltonia asteroides

9 Cimicifuga racemosa (Bugbane)
10 Thalictrum flavum subsp. glaucum (Meadow rue)
11 Aruncus dioicus 'Kneiffii' (Goatsbeard)
12 Polemonium caeruleum (Jacob's ladder)
13 Verbascum nigrum (Mullein)
14 Viola cornuta (Violet)
15 Penstemon barbatus
16 Tropaeolum tuberosum 'Ken Aslet'
17 Mimulus guttatus (Musk)

18 Phygelius x rectus 'Salmon Leap'
19 Campanula latifolia var. macrantha
20 Malva moschata (Musk mallow)
21 Geum rivale 'Lionel Cox'
22 Artemisia lactiflora 'Guizhou' (Mugwort)
23 Jasminum beesianum (Jasmine)
24 Fragaria 'Pink Panda' (Strawberry)
25 Aster divaricatus
26 Salvia patens
27 Dianella ensifolia

74

28 Heuchera 'Plum Pudding' (Coral flower)
29 Corydalis flexuosa 'Père David'
30 Francoa sonchifolia (Bridal wreath)
31 Nepeta sibirica (Catmint)
32 Clematis heracleifolia (Traveller's joy)
33 Inula hookeri
34 Helianthus decapetalus (Sunflower)
35 Chelone obliqua (Turtlehead)
36 Campanula alliariifolia
37 Rudbeckia laciniata (Coneflower)

38 Sidalcea 'Rose Queen' (False mallow)
39 Thalictrum cultratum
40 Penstemon 'Blackbird'
41 Liatris spicata 'Floristan Weiss' (Gayfeather)
42 Digitalis ferruginea (Foxglove)
43 Scabiosa columbaria (Pincushion)
44 Salvia bulleyana
45 Phygelius x rectus 'Winchester Fanfare'
46 Veronica longifolia (Speedwell)

47 Scabiosa 'Miss Willmott'
48 Salvia buchananii
49 Geum 'Georgenberg'
50 Geranium 'Crûg Star'
51 Lonicera periclymenum (Honeysuckle/ Woodbine)
52 Taxus baccata (Yew)

Illustration not to scale

Country houses of the 16th and 17th centuries were likely to have had an orchard and a nuttery. Fanshawe Gate has a large orchard, although many of the trees are old and unproductive. We came up with the idea of starting a nuttery when we were researching replacement trees for the orchard and, as so often happens, the novel idea got more attention than the maintenance task. Forgetting the apple and pear trees, we decided to plant a new fruit or nut tree in the garden for each grandchild. So far, we have a walnut, mulberry and medlar for the first three granddaughters, and fig trees for two grandsons. However, the production of grandchildren is now threatening to overcrowd the garden with trees, so we have turned once again to the orchard. Two more granddaughters and a grandson have been born in the meantime, and we hope to find a new or unusual variety of fruit tree for each one.

Each tree has a little plaque so that the children can find them when they learn to read (and I hope that reading horticultural names at a young age will be a good influence). The plaques look very professional, but, as with all the labelling we do for open days, they expose our knowledge to scrutiny. I used to be very nervous about this, but I have learned that gardeners spot mistakes in a generous spirit and I am happy to learn from them, even though my heart rate might go up at the time. A visitor on one open day pointed out that the tree we had labelled as a quince was, in fact, a medlar. Writing this reminds me that I must make an effort to change the plaque before our next open day.

Our most adventurous excursion into gardening history has been the introduction of different forms of topiary. The garden at Fanshawe Gate is at its most spectacular in mid-summer, when the profuse planting dominates even the strongest stone structures. At other times of year, in winter and early spring especially, the bare bones of the garden's architecture are more apparent. The topiarised plants have introduced a sort of green sculpture, which keeps some visual excitement in the garden throughout the year. Of all our innovations, topiary has had perhaps the most radical effect on the appearance of the garden.

Becoming more widespread in England from the 16th century, topiary recalls an earlier European tradition of gardening, with an emphasis on shape and space. At Fanshawe Gate we have used clipped yews to echo the stone acorns and spheres of the gateposts, or to punctuate a terrace. In English hands, topiary is often entertainingly frivolous, cut into flamboyant shapes such as spirals and waterfalls. Examples of both of these can be seen at Fanshawe Gate.

Mulberry, walnut and medlar trees have been planted recently in the Elizabethan garden, with fig trees against the rear wall.

Topiary acorn and balls echo the shape of the gateposts.

Yew clipped into spirals, cones, balls, and a fountain.

The planting and care of the topiary has been entertaining for us in a different sense. When we arrived in 1959, two yew trees had already been planted on the terrace by the previous owners. The strange thing about trees with slow growth rates is that, seeing them every day, you don't realise how large they are getting. Then one day, perhaps returning from a holiday, you notice that the garden has become quite lopsided. Our two yews had reached the level of the bedroom windows, and were bulking out to occupy a good part of the terrace before we recognised how they dominated the garden. As we had neglected the trees for years, they had died out in the middle while putting on ever more growth round the edges. Our first job was to cut out the dead bits from the centre, using an industrial vacuum to clean them out. Then we wrapped wire round each tree, and four of us pulled hard until we had corseted the tree into a roughly conical shape. We then clipped any bits that still stuck out, until the tree looked slim and sleek once more.

We were so proud of our efforts that we thought we could repeat them on an overgrown conifer in the Elizabethan garden. This tree was in good health but was far too large for its surroundings. We threw a strawberry net over it, tied it in tightly, and then started to pick foliage through the gaps. Our clever idea was that the tree would wear a permanent hairnet, which would remain as an invisible frame beneath the outer growth. But after several hours of teasing greenery through the tiny holes in the net, we got tired and bored. We got out the chainsaw and chopped the tree down. Since the conifer was, in fact, a Leyland cypress, I'm surprised we went to the trouble of trying to beautify it before finally despatching it.

Now under control, the larger yews need clipping only once a year, in spring. The more ornate pieces of topiary need regular haircuts to keep their definition. I use a pair of shears, rather like sheep shears, that can be held in one hand. I try to avoid cutting in bright sunshine, in case the yew scorches.

We started to extend our topiary collection with spirals of box by the front door and in the corners of the terrace, where they provide a pleasing, curvy contrast with the newly conical yew trees. We might have stopped there had we not been to the Chelsea Flower Show and seen the Romantic Garden Nursery's winning display. In great excitement we found an excuse to travel to Norfolk so that we could visit their nursery.

On that first visit we restricted ourselves to buying two bushes which reminded me of clipped poodles. However, we spotted several other attractive shapes, and before long we returned with a borrowed van to buy a fountain-shaped yew tree and two others, clipped into acorn shapes topped by two balls. I then found, as I often do after losing my head in a nursery, that I could not fit everything into the van. The only solution seemed to be to cut the top ball off the bushes. John Powles, the nursery's owner, and his manager, John Carrick, were horrified and refused to let me mutilate the plants they had taken years to grow. So we drove all the way back to Derbyshire with my head sandwiched between two balls of yew. When we got home, we saw that the plants perfectly echoed the stone acorns and balls on the top of the gateposts. It's a very good thing that I did not get my own way.

One other major construction effort in topiary was the planting of a knot garden on the site of our old vegetable plot at the lower entrance to the Cottage. I drew up the design myself, so it is probably not authentic in an historical sense. We planted the knot in two different types of box in order to bring out the illusion of intertwining strands. There is the dark glossy green *Buxus sempervirens* 'Suffruticosa' and the lighter, variegated *Buxus sempervirens* 'Marginata' syn. 'Aureomarginata'. Our funds would not run to planting at intervals of nine inches, so we decided to plant at 18 inch intervals and fill in the gaps the following year. We did not realise that there are variations in the shade of even ordinary box, so our later purchases accidentally added a tapestry effect to the intricacies of the knot.

In the first few seasons we clipped with great care along the lines of boards clamped up hard against the box hedge and adjusted by spirit level. Now that the knot pattern is well established, we can do intermediate trims by eye (usually in rain at the last minute on the night before an open day), with just one annual check with boards and clamps that things are not creeping out of kilter. After the first year we planted box cones at each corner of the knot garden to make the structure more obvious to careless drivers, since, unfortunately, we have to park our cars nearby. It has not worked, and there is at least one cone which is destined never to lead an upright life. There have also been some minor casualties within the knot garden, which has been taken over as a playground by young rabbits. If you look closely, you can see where they have carved out tunnels and archways as they have made the knot garden their own.

Topiary brings the garden to life in winter.

John Pitts trimming the central box cone in the knot garden.

6 mixed borders

In high summer, Fanshawe Gate is transformed into a richly planted cottage garden. Many of the plants are treasured gifts, or recall happy memories. Looking after herbaceous borders is hard but rewarding work. Wooden edgings to the lawns have saved much time and effort, but double digging turned out to be a mistake. The most important contributor to the health of the plants is manure, applied each year by the ton.

I am always surprised by the speed with which the quiet spaces of spring fill up as the garden starts to come into flower. By mid-June, when we begin our open days, Fanshawe Gate has taken on the feel of a cottage garden. The richness of this mixed planting suits the house as much as the more restrained lines of the topiary do in winter, but the season of bright colour and scent is short lived in the Pennine climate.

Not that the garden is completely dormant in winter. The 'Pink Perpetue' rose on the south-facing wall of the house has flowered on Christmas Day almost every year since we planted it in 1960. On Christmas morning all the children used to drag their sacks of presents into our bedroom. After the wrapping paper chaos had subsided, I would open the window for some fresh air, and would usually find one or two blooms of 'Pink Perpetue' nearby, perhaps dusted with frost or a little snow. Last year we pruned the rose harder than usual, and I thought sadly that there would be no Christmas blooms. I was astonished to find one when I opened the window. It was a plastic rose, wired up to the wall on Christmas Eve by my thoughtful husband.

Later in the year, closer to its normal flowering time, the 'Pink Perpetue' rose supports a *Clematis* 'Jackmanii'. Both of these climbers have to be defended against the encroachment of a Virginia Creeper, which is so vigorous that, if we did not cut it back hard every spring, it would soon cover the whole house.

Most of our herbaceous borders are put to sleep for the winter, but the beds which surround the house are planted for interest throughout the year. The south-facing bed which is home to the 'Pink Perpetue' rose and other climbers comes to life in mid-winter with the first snowdrops. I fell in love with a species of giant snowdrop, *Galanthus* 'Sam Arnott', which I saw in the garden of friends who specialised in them. I immediately ordered several clumps and then just as quickly cut my order to one when I saw the price. However, over the past ten years, the snowdrops have multiplied and been divided several times, so restraint and patience were rewarded. Some have been transplanted to the shady part of the Elizabethan garden, where each year they are forgetfully mown, and each year we wait anxiously to see if they will survive.

The snowdrops are complemented by various hellebores, including *Helleborus foetidus* 'Wester Flisk', a present from one of my colleagues in the WRVS. There is an unnamed but pretty *H. orientalis*, and my favourite, *H.* 'Ballard's Black'. This was bought

Rosa 'Pink Perpetue'.

Snowdrops in the woodland border.

87

Top: Paeonia officinalis 'Rubra Plena'.
Centre: Allium cristophii.
Bottom: Pelargonium 'Vancouver Centennial'.

for me by a friend many years ago from Helen Ballard's nursery in Malvern. The hellebores seed prolifically, and we usually have lots of cross-pollinated ones for sale at open days. In March, clumps of miniature *Narcissus* 'Little Wench' and 'Tete à Tete' emerge at the front of the border. They are followed in April by *Erythronium oregonum*, *Tulipa greigii* 'Oratorio', with its showy green and maroon striped leaves, and the beautifully fragrant *Viburnum carlesii*. As spring moves into summer, the full cottage garden planting emerges. There is the old red peony - *Paeonia officinalis* 'Rubra Plena' - which we split from a clump when we first came to Fanshawe Gate. Then there are delphiniums, day-lilies, thistles, catmint, geraniums - especially 'Johnson's Blue' - hostas, and of course foxgloves and the stately hollyhock, *Alcea rosea*, which have self seeded happily throughout the other plants. Mingled with these are the striking accents of *Euphorbia polychroma*, flag iris, Turk's cap lilies, and *Allium cristophii*.

To the left of this bed is a smaller one immediately below the kitchen window. Here is the last remaining trace of my grandfather's bedding-out heritage, the only border where polyanthus and wallflowers still brighten up the late winter months. In summer this bed contains the interesting *Pelargonium* 'Vancouver Centennial'. This may be presumptuous, but I think that this is a plant where nature (or, to be fair to nature, possibly the breeder) made an artistic mistake. 'Vancouver Centennial' has brilliant scarlet flowers which clash violently with its spectacular bronze leaves. But this plant intrigues me, and I have discovered that the maple-shaped leaves look quite attractive underplanted with silver lamium, so I have found a compromise. I simply pick off the flowers and throw them away.

Moving round the courtyard, we have an east-facing border dedicated mainly to roses, and to the moisture-loving plants which surround the pool from the waterfall. As this is one of the routes into the house, and a favourite place to sit for afternoon tea, the scent and glamour of the roses is constantly appreciated. And these roses really do feel glamorous, because we have moved on from neat beds of identical roses, in the style of the 1950s and 1960s, to a looser, more luxuriant style using mixtures of shrub and climbing roses. One of my favourite roses is here: the lovely large-flowered climbing rose 'Constance Spry'. I love this rose for its pink, blowsy cabbage rose appearance, and also for its name. Constance Spry inspired a whole generation of flower arrangers,

Lonicera periclymenum, 'Serotina'.

and usefully taught me that a bowl of beautiful flowers in a tidy room will distract attention from dust and threadbare upholstery. I still have a copy of one of her first books, its pages rippled from water splashes and stained with faded green smudges of flower-arrangers' 'Oasis'.

We have trained roses at different heights, keeping some at waist level, and growing others up steel pillars. The effect of the greater vertical height is to create a tapestry of colour and shape. The pillars support *Rosa* 'Blush Noisette' and *R.* 'Coral Dawn' planted with *Clematis* 'Beauty of Worcester'; *Rosa* 'Desprez à Fleur Jaune' planted with *Clematis* 'Etoile Violette'; and *Rosa* 'Paul's Scarlet Climber' planted with *Clematis x fargesioides* 'Paul Farges'. The rose pillars themselves were the work of Ron Cottyn, who made them during his retirement from a lifetime's work in the Sheffield steel industry. They are beautifully crafted, but like many things in this garden, they are not all they seem. The metal spheres which top each pillar are in fact old ballcocks, painted black.

The wall behind this border is a perfect place for climbers. A *Vitis vinifera* 'Purpurea' contrasts well with the 'Constance Spry' rose. *Clematis orientalis* (the 'orange peel' clematis) has spread over the waterfall lion's head, and other spaces are vigorously filled by *Ceanothus arboreus* 'Trewithen Blue', and *Lonicera periclymenum* 'Serotina'. There is an old rambler rose, 'American Pillar', which we inherited when we came to Fanshawe Gate, and an unidentified rambler which flowers each year from a small crevice high up the wall.

As I have devoted more time to gardening, I have tried to focus on themes for each grouping of plants, be it historical interest, colour, variegation or shape. However, the discipline of absolute consistency is beyond me. John Pitts tried very hard, but there are certain plants which I will not part with, even if their position threatens the integrity of a carefully thought-out design. These are my 'memory' plants; cuttings collected on travels, or gifts from friends and my family, and they mean more to me than any others. Many of the roses were presents, or planted simply because I loved them and had to find a place for them. So one of my favourites, *Rosa* 'Fantin-Latour' stands behind the garden seat by the waterfall, where its sweet, strong perfume cannot be missed. The intensely fragrant standard 'The McCartney Rose' sits just outside the kitchen door for the same reason. Other roses include 'Heritage', 'English Miss', and 'Gertrude Jekyll', chosen because I liked the suggestion of gardening tradition in their names. 'Silver Anniversary', 'Ruby Wedding', and 'Dearest' are self-explanatory. 'Whisky Mac' and 'Glenfiddich' have a place, not for the reason you might expect (I have never been a great drinker), but because I love their colours.

Memory plants also form the fixed points of the herbaceous borders which surround the main lawn and skirt the lower courtyard.

One of the first gifts I planted, in 1960, was a lilac from Betty Mulcrone, the redoubtable midwife at the Jessop Hospital in Sheffield, who delivered four of the children and became an honorary aunt to the family. The lilac was a welcome addition to the border at the north end of the lawn. Although this border was planted in the early 1960s according to a plan from Notcutts, it always seemed a little sparse, and rather too heavy on spotted laurel and *Viburnum tinus*. We redesigned the border only three years ago to include more sun-loving plants, among them *Campanula lactiflora* 'Lodden Anna', *Macleaya cordata, Telekia, Kolkwitzia amabilis, Neillia thibetica, Abelia schumannii, Phlox paniculata* 'Norah Leigh' and 'Harlequin'. There are several geraniums, salvias, eryngiums and a *Lavatera* 'Barnsley'. I have also planted *Fragaria* 'Pink Panda', and the pretty April flowering *Viola* 'Freckles'.

Woodthorpe Hall framed in bronze hazel and beech.

In the meantime, a few more memory plants have been introduced. There is a *Rosa rugosa* from Peter Ball, father of one of my sons-in-law. His former garden at Allen's Green in Hertfordshire was a true plantsman's garden, and is the source of many interesting bulbs at Fanshawe Gate, some of them collected on expeditions in Turkey and North Africa. Then there is a gorgeous white peony, which came from Moscow, where it grows in the dacha garden of Galina, a Russian friend of my eldest daughter, Nicola. I have no idea what it is, but visitors often spot it and ask me about it. Russia has been open to the West for such a short time that it is quite possible that this is a variety unknown in England. Nicola also gave me two roses: 'Nevada', and 'Blanc Double de Coubert'. A weeping pear, *Pyrus salicifolia* 'Pendula', was a Silver wedding present from friends. I have moved it three times, trying to find the best position. It has survived being moved, but has protested by not putting on much growth.

The Russian peony.

This border is now very colourful in summer, and we have planted a yew hedge to give it all a solid backdrop. We planted a bronze hazel and a beech shrub in 1959, which are both now over 10 feet tall. We recently wired them together to form an arch across the entrance to the steps which link the lawn with the lowest level of the garden. The archway has created a fascinating optical effect, framing the only view down the valley towards Sheffield from the garden. Caught in the frame, as if in a painting, is Woodthorpe Hall, the 17th century house which was partly built with materials from Fanshawe Gate.

The path through the hazel and beech archway drops steeply below the steps, and in autumn turns into a lethal, garden version of the Cresta Run, carpeted with hundreds of bullet-hard pears which roll like ball bearings under unwary feet. I am at the age when I would do anything to avoid sliding down a hill on my bottom, but I would not go so far as to remove the old pear tree, which supports a *Rosa filipes* 'Kiftsgate' and is an important feature of the west-facing border above.

This border contained for many years an assortment of perennials, some given, some grown from cuttings. It runs down the entire eastern side of the lawn, broken only by a pathway leading to the Cottage. In the autumn of 1999 we completely overhauled the bed, introducing more of my favourite, cottage garden-type plants, such as day-lilies, delphiniums and campanulas. Three campanulas I particularly like are *Campanula carpatica; C.* 'Burghaltii', with its tubular flowers; and *C. glomerata* 'Superba', which has clusters of bell-shaped flowers. There is a mallow, *Malva moschata,* and several varieties of achillea: *A. filipendulina* 'Gold Plate', *A.* 'Moonshine', and *A. millefolium* 'Cerise Queen'. The Jerusalem sage*, Phlomis fruticosa,* provides beautiful seed heads for flower arranging.

In an herbaceous border like this, bare patches do sometimes appear, and call for a little cheating. I grow lilies in pots, and simply tuck them beneath the foliage of the plants, moving them round as necessary.

The unidentified astrantia.

The double border leading to the dovecote entrance.

Most of the plants in this border are well known, but one is not, and it never fails to catch the eye of visiting plantsmen. It is an astrantia, whose origins I cannot remember. I thought that it was *Astrantia major* 'Shaggy'. Several experts have confirmed that it is not, but no-one has identified it as any other type, although its large, green and white flowers are quite distinctive. I have split the original clump several times and filled in bare spots around the borders. I am beginning to wonder whether we have produced *A. major* 'Fanshawe Gate', and perhaps one day I will find the time to take the plant to Wisley to check whether it is as exciting as I think it is.

Several memory plants remain in this border: a lilac from my youngest daughter, a thank-you gift after her 21st birthday party, and a tree peony, *Paeonia delavayi* var. *ludlowii* from a friend, Jane Greetham, who gave me the seedling from her garden. As the peony grew, I realised that I had planted it in the wrong position, but just as I was about to move it, Jane fell seriously ill. For three months a group of her friends met with her husband to pray for her, and her full recovery a year later seemed miraculous to all of us. I couldn't bring myself to move the peony until Jane was well again, and then we dug a huge hole for it and filled it with fresh soil. It still thrives, producing lovely ebony-black seed pods, which make wonderful presents for gardeners.

At the south end of this border, where it approaches the dovecote, we have planted a yew hedge, parallel with the stone wall of the Elizabethan garden. As it grows, this hedge will enclose a walkway into the dovecote. Between the yew hedge and the path we have made a border which is a double to the dovecote lawn border, and contains the same variety of old plants.

The mixed border in the lower courtyard, near the knot garden, consists almost entirely of gifts or other plants with some sort of personal significance. *Tulipa turkestanica* from Peter Ball are planted beneath a willow, which I grew from a twig taken from the Easter garden in Holmesfield church. An interesting collection of hellebores - many from Helen Ballard's nursery - all came from friends, as did the Pacific Coast irises, the veronica, and the Japanese anemones. The honeysuckle was gathered on holiday in the New Forest - I think it is the common *Lonicera periclymenum*, which we found growing in a hedgerow - and the delphiniums grew from seed bought at Chelsea Flower Show. The 'Madame Butterfly' rose is the same rose that I had in my wedding bouquet in 1952, and 'Royal Volunteer' was named for the 50th anniversary of the WRVS. I also have plants from the most inspired gardens I have visited: *Salvia*

The tree peony in bloom.

Philadelphus 'Belle Etoile' in flower behind the knot garden in the lower courtyard.

Argyranthemum frutescens.

cacaliifolia from Rosemary Verey's garden, a white argyranthemum from Sissinghurst, and a santolina from Beth Chatto. The *Philadelphus* 'Belle Etoile' was in bloom in July 1994 when my youngest daughter was married, and the smell each summer reminds me of that wedding day.

Fanshawe Gate is not a low maintenance garden, and the sheer volume of herbaceous planting means that we spend a lot of time keeping it under control. I don't believe in gardens being sparsely tidy. I like the feeling of exuberant planting on the point of bursting into riot, but supported and restrained where necessary to keep some balance and harmony. The restraining touch need only be a light one, but in this sort of garden it must be done. It needn't require forests of plastic either. I admit that, for years, we used commercially produced plastic supports. Their clever interlocking systems seemed to us a great advance on bamboo canes and string, and we once made a round trip of 150 miles to fill our car boot with factory 'seconds'; they kept us going for ages. Now I have reverted to more natural - and cheaper - methods. When we go out walking in winter, I take a pair of secateurs in my rucsac and prune a few twiggy bits from hazel trees. I cut them to different lengths, and store them until the summer, when I use them to support plants from about nine inches in height. They can be re-used year after year and the plants grow naturally into and around them. I also use supple willow stems bent in an inverted 'U' shape to stop plants at the front of borders flopping on to lawns and paths. A certain amount of flopping is very attractive, but we have to be practical about this, especially when it is time to mow the lawns; the most dangerous task I have ever undertaken in the garden has been to hold up the catmint while John mows the grass beneath it.

On the subject of lawns, I have always thought them very important as a foil for planting, a cool green sea between the islands of colour. But I am not ambitious for bowling green perfection, and I certainly don't have the time to achieve it. I can tolerate some weeds and moss in the lawn, so long as the overall effect is still green. John and Mark, on the other hand, are fanatical about the purity and regularity of the lawns. I think it must be a man thing; I remember my father had the same obsession. As a result of this, we are very strict about mowing the grass, and trimming the edges. This can take hours on the day before an open day, and is the cause of great tension in case it rains.

We are always looking for ways of reducing the burden of chores like this, and the best investment we ever made was to spend one spring sinking wooden edgings around the lawns and grass verges, especially where they border a path. It is surprising how much the appearance of a patchy lawn can be improved if the edges are neat. We used treated wooden boards fixed on edge just below the level of the grass. Very observant visitors might notice that the boards are marked in red in places. The marks show the line of the mains water pipe, which we pierced twice when driving in pegs. The time and cost of repairing the water pipes added unexpectedly to the original investment, but now that we have these firm edges, trimming the grass takes only a few moments as the shears slide easily along the line of the wood.

As I have mentioned in earlier chapters, we spend much time and effort improving the soil and keeping it healthy. We follow an annual routine of mulching and fertilising with farm manure. We consume great quantities of manure, mainly from cows and sheep overwintered in farm buildings nearby: we may take up to 30 tons each year. We store the manure behind the barn in a large pile, and bring it into the garden in one-ton loads on our dumper truck, (the boys' teenage toy, still going strong). Farmyard manure should be rotted for at least five years but I confess that our needs are so great that it has sometimes gone onto our beds not long after it was scraped out of the barn. For this reason we avoid horse manure (although it is wonderful for roses) because horses do not break down seeds in their stomachs and their manure therefore tends to produce more weeds.

We give the beds a top-dressing of manure in the spring, ideally applied in wet weather. The animals seem to love this, and the dog's breath can smell appalling after she has chewed her way through a few choice lumps. Only a light dressing is needed; too much can over-stimulate green growth and reduce flowering. In the late autumn we 'put the beds to sleep' with a two inch deep mulch of woodchip and leaf mould. When we first did this we didn't realise that wood chippings must be rotted for at least a year, otherwise they leach nitrogen from the soil as they decompose. I once tried a mulch of cocoa shell, but it was expensive and its overpowering chocolate smell reminded me disconcertingly of my years working at Cadbury's in Bourneville. The autumn mulching protects plants from frost in winter and helps to keep the soil moist in spring and summer. It also keeps weeds down, and makes it much easier to pull out the few weeds

Lawns are a man thing.

installing wooden lawn edges

The grass edges around the entrance driveway and borders had become ragged and were difficult to maintain.

The new edge is cut along the line of a wooden board.

Treated timber strips are fixed with long wooden pegs along the edge of the grass.

The old grass is replaced with new turf laid on fresh soil and sand.

For smaller, island beds, the wooden edging is nailed together and lifted into position in one piece.

Edgings can also be curved by making a series of saw cuts along the inside face of the timber.

which appear in spring. The only problem is that birds scrabble around in it for nesting material, and by the spring most of the mulch has disappeared.

While I can see the benefits of our annual manuring and mulching routine, I have doubts about the need for deep digging. I used to think that it was the only way of improving our soil, and certainly there are areas where some digging is the only way of breaking up the soil if it has become compacted. In the early years I longed to have the time to do some proper double digging, down to two spade depths. But when we finally got round to it, the result was disastrous. We should have stopped at one spade depth, or taken more care to keep the topsoil and subsoil separate, but instead we brought up shale and clay to the surface and buried the good soil almost two feet underground. I sometimes wonder how the soil would be now if we had adopted a long term 'no dig' approach. I have noticed how quickly the bulky manure is drawn down into the soil by worms, and I suspect that over the course of several years this is all that is needed to maintain good healthy soil.

Another area where we should not have disrupted the soil structure so radically is the vegetable garden. The vegetable garden is really Mark's domain. Like my grandfather, he loves neat rows of vegetables. He also inherited his great-grandfather's obsession with getting stones out of the soil. He laboured for many days, picking out stones and sieving the soil, and looking forward to getting his carrots and parsnips to grow show-bench straight. A year or two on, I think that he would ruefully admit his mistake: the soil has become claggy and drains badly, and he will probably have to labour for a few more days to add grit back to the soil.

Although we are moving steadily towards organic methods, I do often take short cuts, resorting to quick-fix chemical solutions such as a few handfuls of 'Growmore', and fortnightly spraying with 'Roseclear' to keep the hollyhocks free of rust. (If rust does appear, I pull off affected leaves and burn them.) The only other major disease I have to contend with is powdery mildew on the Michaelmas daisies. However, I find that the simplest solution here is to avoid growing too many Michaelmas daisies.

Gill Buck, 1998.

7 quiet corners

The garden at Fanshawe Gate is divided by stone walls into secluded and peaceful areas. The walled Elizabethan garden, the lower courtyard and the stackyard have regained a sense of quiet timelessness since their farming days, but the soil still yields relics of past inhabitants. There are many half-hidden corners to explore or quiet places to sit, from the kitchen courtyard with its sun-baked herbs to the cool, ferny shade of the woodland borders.

We were lucky that the basic structure of the garden at Fanshawe Gate was already a series of compartments, mainly divided by stone walls. It is one of those gardens where views are partially screened, where paths wind out of sight and doorways reveal a glimpse of a hidden landscape to be explored beyond.

If you stand on the main lawn, you can see the fruit trees of the orchard, rising above the wall which separates the rough meadow grass from the rest of the garden. The heads of people up in the vegetable garden, or the tips of the runner bean supports might be just visible above the courtyard wall. Turning north, you see the yew hedge which screens the long stone roof of the old tithe barn in the stackyard below the house. To the south, an old stone wall divides the lawn across its entire width. In the centre, a doorway invites you to walk through into the Elizabethan garden.

The Elizabethan garden only has its name because of a whim of John's when we first moved to Fanshawe Gate; he thought it seemed the most authentically historic part of the garden. In fact, old photographs show it as part of a working farm early in the 20th century, almost covered by a giant haystack. Nevertheless, it has easily recovered a sense of quiet timelessness, separated from the rest of the garden by walls at head height. This is the place to sit in high summer, when the walls throw back the sun's heat, and the surrounding trees provide shade. The enclosed space concentrates your view, and makes the principal border an ideal spot for our experiment in variegated plants.

My grandfather's old summer house stands in one corner of the Elizabethan garden, and we still gather in front of it for afternoon tea, just as we did when I was a child. It's a strange feeling to see its hexagonal form and thatched roof in the background of faded family photographs: myself, my sister and cousins in the children's clothes of the 1930s. The people have changed, but the summer house has survived everything, including rescue in the 1970s from Grandfather's abandoned garden. It lost its thatch and was recovered with roofing felt tiles by my Uncle Jack. When it came to Fanshawe Gate, we decided against re-thatching it on the grounds that thatch is not a local material.

The summer house was one of Grandfather's bargains. He always bought in bulk, and could not resist a good deal. He spotted the summer house at the Norton show, near Sheffield, and noticing that the manufacturer came from Devon, offered £30 instead of the £40 asking price to save the seller carting it all the way back home.

The summer house at Aston Mount in 1938. Cynthia Ramsden is in the second row on the left.

The summer house at Fanshawe Gate in 2001.

103

The vegetable garden is hidden away above the main garden.

A stream runs beneath trees opposite the house.

So far as I know, he only bought one summer house, which is perhaps surprising. The oak and chrome tubs which held his spring bulbs were bought as a lot of fifty, even though only a few of them could fit into the bay windows of the drawing room. He once bought several Aga kitchen ranges (in their first generation of fashion), and delivered them to each of his children, who didn't have much choice in the matter. My parents' tiny kitchen consisted of a huge Aga and not much else. His style was an odd combination of largess and parsimony. Only recently I learned from my cousin Geoffrey that Grandfather saved the small stones we picked out of the borders in order to build a new wall at the end of the garden.

When we came to Fanshawe Gate, the Elizabethan garden was, like the rest of the place, home to beds of dahlias, with walls covered in Russian vine. We made our changes slowly, replacing the dahlias with roses, and leaving in place a slope of overgrown laurel bushes, which made a wonderful climbing frame and hiding place for the children. After many years, we felt the need for more radical change, and removed the laurels and some conifers, which had become oppressive.

Old photographs show a very open aspect to the Elizabethan garden, but over the course of the last century the surrounding trees have grown enormously. There are several dark and shaded areas, and these have made a natural home for shrubs we brought from our suburban garden in Sheffield: holly, rhododendrons, cotoneaster and laburnum. To brighten things up, we planted a silver birch, which has done well in the wooded setting. You may be surprised - there being no doubt now about my hatred of this plant - that *Aegopodium podagraria* 'Variegatum', the variegated ground elder, continues to grow beneath the trees. Frankly, I haven't the energy to dig it out. It does its duty, lighting up the dark corners. Provided it continues to behave itself in the shade, I shall allow it to stay. Ferns also thrive here, and have spread around the ancient stone staddle stones.

The Elizabethan garden runs alongside the lane. On the other side of the lane, there is a small, shady area which is neither completely wild, nor quite part of the garden. Years ago, the local council gave us permission to reseed the grass verge and to plant bulbs beneath the trees. We put a bench by the stream for walkers to rest. The children's favourite playground was here, climbing trees and treasure hunting in the stream. They found bits of pottery and clay pipes, and even pieced together the whole of a glass bowl commemorating Queen Victoria's Diamond Jubilee. I have also found some interesting things in the garden, and when I lose something myself I often wonder whether it will reappear in fifty or a hundred years' time, under the spade of a future gardener. I have found coins - the oldest dated 1815 - and brooches. One of these is a silver 'Mother' brooch (I hope she wasn't too sad at losing it), and the other is a 'Mizpah' brooch. This find made me wonder about the fate of whoever lived at Fanshawe Gate in the early years of the 20th century, since these brooches were often given by serving men to their wives and sweethearts. The word 'Mizpah' refers to the Old Testament, Book of Genesis Ch13 v. 49 when Jacob and Laban made a covenant, witnessed by God, that neither would take advantage of the other in their absence. The meaning must have carried huge significance for couples separated by war: 'May the Lord keep watch between you and me when we are away from each other'. I wonder whether the loss of the brooch tells us anything about the effectiveness of this moral chastity belt.

Old kitchen courtyard, 1960.

A favourite quiet corner of mine is the little walled courtyard by the kitchen door. This is where I grow herbs for cooking, in a raised bed which gives impressive height to the rampant angelica, and contains the equally vigorous mint. The high surrounding walls trap the aroma of the herbs and of a honeysuckle, so that I can leave the kitchen door open on summer evenings and enjoy the snatches of scent while I cook supper. Unfortunately, the kitchen extractor also blows into this little courtyard, and those sitting outside don't really appreciate the reversal of the scents, even when it's roast lamb.

It's important to grow herbs as close as possible to the kitchen. A few years ago, all our herbs grew in the lower courtyard, where the knot garden now stands. In the cold weather, no one wanted to trek across the wet lawn and down the slippery path to collect herbs. An effort was usually made, however, for sage. One of our favourite autumn Sunday lunches was roast pork with apple sauce and season pudding. The children could usually be persuaded to put on their wellingtons to collect apples from the orchard and sage from the herb garden for the season pudding. Season pudding is a traditional accompaniment to roast pork in the North, a sort of Yorkshire pudding with sage and onion.

The kitchen courtyard.

Roast pork and season pudding.

I have the recipe from my grandmother, who thought in handfuls and pinches rather than weights, so, in passing it on to you here, I have tried to estimate the modern measures. Although the pudding is made of a batter flavoured with sage and onion, it is absolutely unthinkable to substitute a packet of stuffing mix, no matter how short of time you may be.

season pudding

batter	other ingredients
2 eggs	*1 onion, sliced, boiled and chopped up*
3 oz (75g) plain flour	*1 heaped tablespoon porridge oats*
5-6 fluid oz (150-175ml) milk	*1 heaped tablespoon shredded suet*
salt and pepper	*1 heaped tablespoon fresh sage - blanch the leaves in boiling water to bring out the flavour, and chop finely.*

7 x 11 inches (18 x 28cm) baking tin.

The pudding cooks in the oven with the pork for the last hour of the pork's cooking time.

Mix the batter ingredients together, and add the other ingredients. Mix well. Add a drop of cold water if the mixture seems to be too stiff (it should drop softly from the spoon). Pour enough fat from the roasting pork to cover the base of the tin, and heat it on the top shelf of the oven until the fat is smoking hot. Pour in the batter, and return to the top shelf for about one hour. The pudding should be well browned, and crisp round the edges. Cut into squares to serve with the roast pork and apple sauce.

It's a shame that we have forgotten so many traditional uses for herbs, including many which are non-culinary. I remember that we used to make a pleasant-smelling moth deterrent out of dried thyme, dried tansy leaves and powdered cloves (1 tablespoon of each), mixed with two tablespoons each of dried rosemary and dried mint leaves. We would crush them all up, and tie the mixture into little muslin bags to hang in the wardrobe.

A final note on herbs. I remember an old saying that if you could grow parsley, you would wear the trousers in your household. If you want to be sure that your parsley will grow well, pour a kettleful of boiling water over the drill after you have sown the parsley seed. It always seems to work for the parsley, if not for the trousers.

Myra Powell, 1998.

8 potting sheds & greenhouses

The working day begins at sunrise in the potting shed, which was built a few years ago from old stone. Hours pass unnoticed until it is time to move to the greenhouse for tea and the newspapers. Seeds and cuttings flourish in a home-made mist propagator: plants are grown for the garden, or for sale at open days.

It has taken years to build a real potting shed. We now have a stone building between the greenhouse and the main house. Thanks to Mark's hoarding, we were able to use old stone for the walls and roof, and traditional mullions for the window. The potting shed was only built in 1995, but looks as if it has stood there for decades. Stone weathers quickly in the damp Pennine air, although we sometimes speed it up by smearing on a paste of yoghurt and sheep dung. On the wall and over the door I have trained the pink climbing rose 'High Hopes', underplanting it with the purple climber *Rhodochiton atrosanguineus.* I sell a lot of these plants on open days, grown from seeds which I collect in the autumn. In this part of the country *Rhodochiton* usually grows as an annual, but I find that I can lift the root and overwinter it in the greenhouse, and by mid-March it is putting on more growth than the seedlings.

The beds in front of the potting shed are currently filled with the deep crimson rose 'The Prince', which I have on trial from David Austin. When we began the trial in 1997 I was struck by the rose's fragrance, and the way its colour deepens to a rich purple, but I was disappointed by the weight of the flowers, which seem almost too heavy for the stems to support.

In the early years we were never able to find room for a potting shed because we needed space to store coal for the house. There was a glimmer of hope after we put in central heating, and the coal shed seemed to be redundant. Sadly, the oil crisis of 1973 ended our new-found comfort, as we could no longer afford the oil for the boiler. The potting shed was postponed, and on its site we installed an enormous wood-burning stove, large enough to heat the house and hot water. For the next few years we were preoccupied with finding enough wood to feed the stove, which could consume whole tree trunks. In those perhaps more innocent days, John saw nothing wrong with keeping his chainsaw and a boiler suit in the back of the car, ready to seize any opportunity that might appear as he drove to and from work. He was once spotted by a surprised colleague, as he wielded his chainsaw alongside a gang of workmen who were felling a tree. His colleague claimed that John stood out from the rest of the gang because he was still wearing his bowler hat. Apocryphal as that story may be, John certainly had a slightly odd appearance in those years. Every time the stove door was opened to feed in more wood, it let out a blast of searing heat. Over time, John's

Inside the potting shed.

113

eyebrows were singed away and his hair turned a yellowish grey at the front. The potting shed finally became a reality, and John began to look more normal, only after the oil price came down and we switched on our old central heating again.

The potting shed is where I go for five minutes, and leave two hours later. The grandchildren call it my pottering shed, and they are absolutely right. It is where I most want to be at 6 o'clock on a spring or summer morning, drinking tea while I watch the sun rise over the garden. It is where I plan and prepare, and start off all the cuttings and seedlings which will eventually be transplanted into the garden or sold through Plant Aid (see later in this chapter) and at our own open days.

The potting shed is not very large: about twelve feet by eight. It has a steel sink, and some workbenches. The tools are thrown into a large box, which falls far short of the standards set by my grandfather's magnificent potting shed. In my grandfather's garden, the last half hour of the gardener's working day was spent washing, drying and oiling his tools, stacking them neatly on their pegs, then sweeping down the stone floor with disinfectant. I remember the gleaming racks of spades, forks, half-moons, rakes and shears, and the neat bundles of bamboo canes. That potting shed smelled heavenly; the air was thick with the warm oiliness of tarred string and the astringent smell of raffia, hanging in well-groomed skeins from big hooks on the wall.

My potting shed contains a more curious mixture of things which I find useful in the garden, and I pass on a list of them here, in the hope that one or two of them may be new to you.

1 net bags

From supermarket fruit. I lift the spring flowering bulbs, such as tulips, and store them in these nets in a cool, airy place - hanging up on the wall is fine - until the autumn. It's useful to label each bag with the name, colour and height of the bulbs.

2 old nylon tights

These are a useful item in the first aid kit for damaged plants. Cut into strips, they are used to bandage up standard roses which snap in a high wind. Bandaged, staked, and watered, such casualties have a good chance of surviving. It goes without saying that it's best to stick to neutral shades of tights.

3 packs of vinyl gloves

To wear when potting up or pricking out. I spend so much time gardening that keeping my hands clean is a real problem (bearing in mind that many of our garden visitors know that I have prepared the food they are eating). Even when I wear gloves, before I put them on I dig my fingers into a bar of soap, until my nails are completely caked. It's then easy to scrub them clean later. For badly ingrained dirt, I pour some olive oil or sunflower oil into the palm of one hand, add a level teaspoon of sugar, and rub my hands together, rinsing off finally under warm water. Sometimes I rub halves of lemons over my fingers. This is an ancient staple of womens' magazine advice for 'softening and whitening' the fingers. It's certainly more pleasant than Aunt Bea's Domestos and Chanel No.5 trick (see Chapter 1).

4 old woollen gloves

Put these on over the vinyl gloves. Dip your fingers into weedkiller gel, and stroke it onto the stems of bindweed and ground elder.

5 plastic bags & newspaper

These are excellent for conserving moisture in clay pots, which can dry out faster than you would like. Before planting, line the pot either with a plastic bag or with wet newspaper. I also keep gravel to cover the surface of pots and ornamental containers. As well as keeping the soil moist, the gravel makes weeding easy and it looks very smart.

6 old plastic bottles

Nowadays it's considered bad practice to reuse household containers in the garden. But I confess that I still do it, because I hate buying and throwing away so much plastic. However, I am very careful about washing things out, labelling containers clearly, and keeping them well out of the reach of children. I use old spray-top window cleaner bottles for misting with water, foliar feed, or insecticide, and I am really parsimonious with old fizzy drink bottles. I cut off the bottom six inches of a bottle, saving the top bit for propagating plants, and I fill it with bleach and water. I then soak white plastic plant labels in this solution for at least a week. A quick rinse and scrub with a Brillo pad gets rid of supposedly indelible ink, and the labels are ready to use again.

The old greenhouse site in 1995 : the greenhouse had been demolished but the vines and peaches continued to grow.

7 paraffin

Not for heating, but for mixing up with water (one tablespoon of paraffin to one pint of water). Soak your spring flowering bulbs in this solution for half an hour before you plant them in the autumn, and with a bit of luck the mice and squirrels won't touch them.

8 jeyes fluid

This is something that has endured from my grandfather's time, and I use it in exactly the same way as he did. Diluted, I brush it onto stone paving, steps and paths, three or four times a year, to prevent them from becoming slippery (a real hazard at Fanshawe Gate). The smell fades quickly, but the liquid stains permanently, so wear old clothes and wellingtons.

9 mothballs & tarred string

I do not have either of these in the potting shed at the moment, but I mention them in case you are able to find some. Both can protect against carrot fly attack: the mothballs crushed up and mixed with sieved soil for planting the carrot seeds, and the tarred string laid between rows of seeds. My grandfather used to lay it in strips between the carrot and cabbage rows.

10 molehills

Collect the soil from molehills, and mix it with some horticultural sand. It makes a lovely aerated tilth for sowing seed and repotting plants, and it is satisfying to turn a nuisance to such advantage.

I pass on one final tip from the potting shed, but cannot claim that it is tried and tested. I once read that, if you can persuade a teenage girl to prepare and plant your cuttings, they will take without any need to use hormone rooting powder. I was never able to test this idea, because my own teenage girls were too busy chasing boyfriends. Nor was I able to check whether male hormones had the same - or any other interesting - effect, since the boys were expending their testosterone racing round on their dumper truck.

The greenhouse is almost as much a sanctuary as the potting shed, and we often sit there to have tea or to read the papers. The rear wall of the greenhouse is in fact a 10-foot high boundary wall, providing protection from the winds sweeping over from the Peak District moorlands. The wall has been scrubbed clean of the limewash from the previous greenhouse, a white painted wooden lean-to. When we came to Fanshawe Gate, we found that the wall in this greenhouse, buffeted by wind on its north-west side, sheltered on the inner, sunny side a peach tree and two vines. I used to pollinate the peach flowers with cotton wool on the end of a bamboo cane; the traditional method is to use a rabbit's tail, but the children wouldn't let me anywhere near their pet bunnies. Although the plant often suffered from peach leaf curl, the peaches themselves were delicious: small and downy, with an intensely sweet flavour. Whenever I bite into a chilled supermarket peach and find flavourless woodiness, I remember our old peaches with nostalgia. The vines - a Black Hamburg and a Muscat - also yielded good fruit in the years when I found time to thin out the bunches. To protect these fruit plants, we had to run paraffin heaters in colder weather, topping them up regularly from late autumn to spring.

The old greenhouse, having taken up many hours of our time with patching and repainting, finally rotted away. At the time, all we wanted was something cheap and convenient to replace it. We bought a small aluminium greenhouse, large enough for a few seed trays and a couple of grow-bags. There was just room to squeeze in our deckchairs for the occasional post-gardening snooze. However, this was not a greenhouse to fall in love with, and we were soon convinced that we would have to build a wooden greenhouse again, on the site of the old one, with materials and proportions in harmony with the garden. In the meantime, the peach had terminally succumbed to peach leaf curl. The vine, growing through the ruins of the old greenhouse, had become far too large to be contained, so we took it out and made a fresh start. The new greenhouse is built of a Malaysian hardwood called balau, which I believe has similar properties to oak. The hardness of the wood made the construction extremely difficult, and it took three different firms of joiners to finish the job.

Plants for sale are arranged on staging outside the new greenhouse.

Family members drafted in to clean up the wall for the new greenhouse.

The new greenhouse gave us a chance to grow much greater quantities of plants from seeds and cuttings. In the early 1990s I had become involved with a project called Plant Aid, organised by my friend and GP, Jill Bethell, and her husband Tony. Plant Aid started as a group of friends who grew their own plants and sold them at a grand sale held each spring in Jill's garden. The sales have become extremely popular, since many of the growers are specialists in particular areas; alpine plants, or vegetables for example. I concentrate on unusual herbaceous plants. Plant Aid has to date raised over £50,000 to support a hospice and other local charities.

I find now that the early part of my gardening year is devoted to preparing plants for Plant Aid, as well as for our open days. We have been surprised by the demand for plants, especially the less well-known ones, and we decided to try to meet it by building a mist propagator in the greenhouse. Since Mark was the driving force behind this project, the mist propagator has turned out to be a contraption of technological ingenuity and almost industrial size. He started by designing a galvanised steel frame almost half the length of the greenhouse and persuading a local engineering firm to fabricate it. Then he put the internal workings together himself, including drainage, heating cables, and a solenoid-fed misting unit. The heating and the misting are controlled independently and the propagator itself is

The greenhouse and potting shed in spring.

divided into two halves which can run at different temperatures. In its first year of operation, Mark used it to start off seedlings for the vegetable garden. None of us realised what a boost to productivity it would be, and we found ourselves awash with hundreds of lettuces.

The mist propagator was quickly discovered by our cats. They are supposed to live in the barn and catch rats, but they spend most of their time warming their tummies on the heated gravel. They usually slink away when they hear me coming, but I can always see their pawmarks in the seed trays.

Delys Fiddes, 2001.

120

Delys Fiddes, 2001

9 wild life

All kinds of animals live in the garden: dogs, cats, ducks, hens and a flock of doves are the domestic residents, while the garden is occasionally threatened by escaping cows, sheep and horses. Smaller pests include foxes, moles, slugs and snails. Some animals are surprising: a badger moved into the house and tried to become a member of the family, while a recent field study revealed the true character of the doves.

It is not easy to draw distinctions between the different animals which inhabit the garden at Fanshawe Gate. The boundary between domestic and wild is often unsure, and the same animal has sometimes been both pet and predator.

Take, for example, our badger. We rarely catch sight of badgers in the garden nowadays, but we know that they visit regularly because they use the borders as their toilet. A few years ago, however, a badger pushed open our front door, walked into the sitting room and sat in front of the fire. We all cautiously climbed back down off the sofa (except the dog, who never came to terms with the visitor), and discovered that this astonishingly domesticated badger was quite friendly. We learned that she was an orphan, found and hand-reared by a neighbour. She visited regularly, eating in the kitchen, and learning to tip over the waste bin and to open doors with her powerful front paws. She took to climbing the stairs, and exploring the bedrooms. We did not always notice her arrival, because the front door was usually open. One night we had visitors and some of the children were in sleeping bags on the floor. When we went to check the children before we went to bed, we found the badger, snuggled down beside our youngest daughter. It was our one moment of real worry; we could cope with fleas, but we did not want to startle the badger by waking her, and risking an attack from her sharp teeth. She was gently coaxed out with the help of a tin of dog food.

After a few months of nightly visits the badger went back to the wild. We noticed that she sometimes arrived with another badger, who stayed in the shadows outside the gate. She had obviously found a mate; her visits gradually ceased. I hope that she reverted to normal badger life, and I like to think that the invisible badgers who leave their mark on our borders at night might be her descendants.

My greatest enemy is the fox. I have loved watching fox cubs play at night, and will never forget an extraordinary moonlit night when John and I saw a large dog fox silhouetted at the top of a field, touching noses with our curious pony. But we keep ducks and hens, and the carnage if the fox gets through our defences is truly stomach-churning. I would be especially sorry to lose our cockerel, Arnold, who is named after Grandfather Biggin. The war against the fox also continues in the garden, where he digs up the lawn in his search for slugs and insects.

On the subject of slugs: I don't like throwing chemicals around (except when quick

Top: Visitors welcome ....
Centre and bottom: ....and less welcome.

results are called for), and prefer to deal with slugs by drowning them in beer and tipping them out into a field. I sink jam jars of beer into the ground near vulnerable plants and I sprinkle crushed egg shells around the plants as an extra precaution. The jam jars also attract earwigs, which is a bonus. I leave out a few piles of drowned slugs from the beer traps on summer evenings, in the hope that the fox will enjoy them and won't bother to dig up the lawn.

A quick solution to slugs and snails is to let the hens and ducks loose in the garden; a real treat for them. The only problem is the damage they do as they furtle through the flower beds. (Furtle is an old Derbyshire word, which describes, among other things, exactly what ducks and hens do in flower beds.)

Squirrels and moles fall into my category of cuddly nuisances; pests which are tolerated because they bring some benefits. The squirrels infuriate me when (despite my paraffin-soaking trick) they dig newly planted bulbs out of troughs and tubs, but I do love watching young squirrels playing on the staddle stones in the woodland area, or trying to steal nuts from the birdfeeder. I read that squirrels often forget where they have stashed their winter food, and may die of starvation as a result. Even though it's against my own best interests, I do sometimes leave a few piles of peanuts out for them.

I am even more fond of moles, although they are constantly ruining the hellebores in the woodland borders. They have not yet discovered the lawn. Even if they do, I could not bring myself to lay traps for them. I find it hard enough to see one of the cats sitting watchfully over a mole hill. I admire the endeavours of moles, the amount of earth they can move with their shovel-like front feet. I am of course very grateful for this beautifully aerated earth, which is carried back to the potting shed for seedlings.

The less cuddly nuisances tend to be escapees from nearby fields: cows, horses, and sheep. We have often woken and drawn back the curtains in the morning to see a herd of large animals quietly churning up the lawn and chewing the plants. However, we did once have a surprisingly helpful sheep invasion when the animals did a good job of pruning the roses. That year I needed to do no more than trim the bushes into shape, and the roses seemed to flourish after this rough treatment. We do in fact invite two well-known sheep to spend a few weeks with us every year. Brian and Stanley, the local tups, spend their off-duty time keeping the grass down in our orchard, much easier for us than struggling with scythes or our old rotary mower.

A distinctive feature of Fanshawe Gate is the flock of fan-tailed doves which live in the old stone dovecote. On a quiet summer's day, the only sounds in the garden may be their gentle cooing and the whistling sound of their wings as they take off and land. The doves are now the most famous inhabitants of Fanshawe Gate, seen on television, in the Radio Times, and the subject of some of the research which underpinned Tim Birkhead's book, 'Promiscuity' (pub. 2000 by Faber). In our ignorance, we had always thought of our doves as symbols of romantic innocence. We had to rethink our ideas about the doves after Professor Birkhead's Ph.D. student, Claire Lovell Mansbridge, finished three years of field study in the garden at Fanshawe Gate, and published her thesis 'Sperm Competition in the Feral Pigeon Columba Livia' in 1995. We had no idea there were such goings-on in the dovecote. Further evidence of the racy home lives of our dear doves was recorded by the BBC's Natural History Unit, for a Valentine's Day programme on pairing and infidelity in the animal kingdom. Appropriately, it was called 'A Wild Romance'.

The most troublesome birds we have are finches, which nip off clematis shoots. Stringing cotton through the plants was not as effective as I had hoped, so I tried another trick; hanging long strips of colourful plastic nearby. I used strips cut from bright yellow fertiliser bags provided by my farming neighbour, tying them to the wires which support the clematis and the climbing roses through which they grow. It was a successful deterrent, but an aesthetic disaster, looking rather like custard dripping down the wall.

Horses, ducks and hens share the stackyard.

Arnold the cockerel was named after Grandfather Biggin.

130

Delys Fiddes, 2001

10 garden open days

The gardening year at Fanshawe Gate is organised around the open days in June and July. Receiving as many as 400 visitors a day relies on a huge voluntary effort, and attention to many details which are nothing to do with gardening. Visitors are given a warm welcome, and treated to home-made teas, with lunch or supper for smaller groups.

Opening the garden to the public is the highlight of our summer. We have always shared our garden, lending it for garden parties and charity events, and have also used it for many family celebrations: christenings, birthday parties, weddings, bonfire parties and so on. But it was not until 1994 that we opened the garden as an object in itself. By then of course most of the children had left home, so I now had the time to work consistently on the garden and to think more about its design. That first open day, for the Derbyshire Wildlife Trust, was such an unexpected success that I began to think about repeating it, perhaps for the National Gardens Scheme. By coincidence I was then contacted by the local organiser for the National Gardens Scheme, and we went ahead with our first opening for them in 1995.

Once in the famous yellow National Gardens Scheme directory, we were drawn into the very British world of gardening passion and voluntary effort. We were contacted by gardening clubs and horticultural societies from all over Britain and Ireland, and even from the USA. We now have two to three visits each week from such groups, in addition to the public open days at weekends. Fanshawe Gate, we learned recently, is one of the most visited private gardens in Derbyshire. I know there are many people who come more than once each year, and I often bump into people at the supermarket checkout whose faces have become familiar from open days. We are close enough to a large city that the garden is an easy destination for a summer afternoon, yet even on the busiest days it still feels remote and peaceful. Some of our visitors are artists, and they have returned at other times to paint or draw. Several of their works have been used to illustrate this book.

In the early years of opening we discovered how much needs to be done apart from work on the garden. We have to decide our entry charge (kept at a very reasonable £1.50); take bookings; put up posters in advance and signs for car parking, loos, and routes round the garden on the day; check the labelling of garden plants and plants for sale; organise stewards for the car park and volunteers to sit at the gate or sell plants; arrange for local jazz or chamber music groups to play in the garden; prepare food and drink and organise volunteers from the WRVS to manage all the serving and washing up.

A garden tour begins in the lower courtyard.

Cynthia guiding one of the many private visits.

Children are especially welcome at open days.

We have become more efficient over the years, but it is still an amateur and voluntary effort. I was amused to see recently that what we do instinctively or by trial and error in order to open our garden was described in a university study as 'Managing the Visitor Experience'. In fact, when I read the list of factors which 'determine the visitor experience', I became more conscious of what makes a garden visit enjoyable. We tear our hair out if rain stops us mowing the lawns before an open day, or if the topiary is looking shaggy, but this is unlikely to put visitors off. Far more important is a friendly welcome, including a welcome for children; a modest entry charge and convenient opening times, helpful signposting round the garden, lots of information, teas and plant sales, and of course a good setting and landscape and plenty to see in season.

Sadly, the most important factor in our visitors' enjoyment is the weather, and that we cannot control. For two days before an open day I watch every weather forecast on television, stay tuned to the radio, and turn first to the weather page in the newspaper. It's not just that fewer people visit in bad weather. Heavy rain can prevent us using the field for parking and create a logistical nightmare, because the lane leading to Fanshawe Gate is too narrow in places for cars to park and easily pass each other. We were initially taken aback by the numbers of visitors. Coping with 200 or so cars was an unforeseen task, and when groups started to arrive in coaches, we realised that we had to devote as much attention to traffic management as to gardening. One large coach all but manoeuvred itself into the pond. So on busy days we hire the Dronfield Community minibus and operate a sort of park and ride service from the Robin Hood Inn at the top of the lane. Many people, once they have got out of their coach, prefer to walk the three quarters of a mile to the house. The road to Fanshawe Gate runs along the spine of a hill, with dramatic views of Sheffield to the north and the Peak moorlands to the south and west. It's a worthwhile walk, mostly downhill, and we make sure that visitors are well fortified with tea before the uphill return.

Which brings me to the subject of catering. Garden visiting in Britain would be unthinkable without at least a cup of tea and a biscuit at some point in the day. I was brought up with strong traditions of hospitable baking, and we expect to serve our guests with scones and home-made jam, shortbread, ginger and hazelnut biscuits, chocolate and coffee sponge cakes, fruit cake, date and walnut loaf, and, of course, Bakewell Pudding. Like everyone else with a Bakewell Pudding recipe,

I believe mine to be the original, and far better than anything you can buy in a shop. I often offer lunch or supper to smaller groups. Because I do all the food preparation myself, I have had to develop a small selection of tasty and completely reliable dishes which can be prepared in advance. I have written out some of these recipes for you (I now know most of them by heart), and I hope that you might enjoy them on a summer's evening with family or friends, even if you are not cooking for a large crowd.

Preparing the food myself is manageable with good planning, but serving it on the day is impossible without lots of help. On a busy Sunday afternoon we might serve tea to as many as 400 people. I rely completely on my old colleagues from the WRVS. These are people who can gauge to the last drop the moment when the tea urn must be refilled; who can cut up cakes with one hand and scoop up a pile of crockery for washing with the other. They never panic. Many of them, like me, are well into their retirement, but they have the stamina to stay on their feet all day. The leader of the team, Jack Thompson, is one of the fittest people I know; in his late seventies, he attempted the climb of Mont Blanc with me in 1999 to raise money for charities. Even with such competent support I still make mistakes, especially in estimating food quantities. Once or twice I've been interrupted when talking to visitors by a message that the teas are running low. When this happens I run to the kitchen and tip a bag of scone mix into the Kenwood mixer (I've no scruples about cheating in these circumstances; the scones taste quite good if you eat them warm). My visitors stand in the kitchen door, and we finish our conversation over the hum of the mixer.

Here are the recipes I use most often.

Jack Thompson preparing afternoon tea.

afternoon tea

plain scones

The following quantities make 12 scones.

8 oz (225g) self-raising flour
1¹/₂ oz (40g) butter
1¹/₂ tablespoons caster sugar
pinch of salt
5 fl oz (150ml) milk

Sift the flour and salt into a bowl, and rub in the butter with your fingertips.

Add the sugar and then the milk, drop by drop, until the mixture is fairly soft. I find it helpful to do the mixing with a knife. Roll the dough onto a floured board to a thickness of ¾ inch (2 cm).

Cut into rounds with a 2 inch (5 cm) pastry cutter, gathering up and re-rolling the remains as necessary. Put the rounds of dough on a greased baking sheet, and brush with a little milk, or some beaten egg mixed with milk. Bake at 220°C (gas mark 7) for 12-15 minutes.

You don't need to leave these to cool for long before eating them, preferably with some thick cream and good strawberry jam.

I can guarantee at least that the first batch of scones on open days will be made this way.

strawberry conserve

As well as being delicious in sponge cakes, making your own strawberry conserve salves the conscience if you have resorted to packet-mix scones.

3 lb (1.35 kg) strawberries
3 lb (1.35 kg) preserving sugar

Layer the strawberries in a large bowl with the sugar. Cover and leave for 24 hours.

Put into a preserving pan and bring slowly to the boil, stirring to dissolve the sugar. Boil rapidly for 5 minutes. Return to the bowl and cover. Leave for 48 hours. Put back into the pan and boil rapidly for 10 minutes.

Leave to cool for 15 minutes, stir, pour into pots, cover and seal.

Tip: If a froth appears on the finished conserve, stir in a small knob of butter and the froth will disappear.

shortbread

8 oz (225 g) butter
4 oz (110 g) caster sugar
12 oz (350 g) plain flour

7 x 11 x 1 inch (18 x 28 x 2.5 cm) baking tin.

Cream the butter and sugar until light and fluffy. Add the flour and mix until a smooth paste is formed. It could hardly be simpler.

Crocosmia 'Lucifer'.

Then, either: roll out on a floured board to not less than ¹/₂ inch (1 cm) thickness. Using a floured cutter, cut into rounds or shapes. Place on a baking tray lined with non-stick baking parchment and bake at 150°C (gas mark 2) for 20 to 30 minutes until firm and golden brown. Remove to a cooling tray and dredge with caster sugar. Leave to cool.

Or: press the mixture into a shallow tin. Level and firm with a palette knife. Make a pattern on the surface with a fork, criss cross or straight lines. Bake as above, but for longer: 30 to 40 minutes. Remove from the oven and cut into fingers while still hot. Dredge with caster sugar. Remove from the tin when cold.

crispy gingerbreads

These are also very quick and easy to make.

4 oz (110 g) margarine
12 oz (350 g) granulated sugar
9 oz (250 g) self-raising flour
2 teaspoons powdered ginger
1 egg

Jack serves lunch.

WRVS helpers prepare to serve supper.

Cream the margarine and sugar, add the beaten egg. Sift the flour and ginger and add to the creamed mixture. Roll into walnut sized balls. Place on a baking tray lined with non-stick silicone baking parchment. Bake at 150°C (gas mark 2) for 15-20 minutes until the surface is cracked and golden brown. Cool slightly before removing to a cooling tray.

bakewell pudding

The original Bakewell Pudding is made with puff pastry. It can seem rather oily, so I feel it needs to be served slightly warm. Here I give two versions: the original, and my grandmother's recipe, which uses a shortcrust pastry. I suppose the latter is really a tart (but don't let anyone in Bakewell hear you call it that).

Collecting entrance money on a National Gardens Scheme open day.

bakewell pudding

6 oz (175 g) puff pastry (buy it ready-made: life's too short to make your own)
3 oz (75 g) butter
4 oz (110 g) caster sugar
3 eggs
1 level tablespoon ground almonds
almond essence
strawberry jam and good lemon curd

8 inch (20 cm) round cake or flan tin

Line the base and sides of the tin with pastry. Cover the bottom with a thin layer of jam and lemon curd mixed. In a saucepan melt the butter, add the sugar. Beat the eggs together and stir into the butter and sugar mixture. Heat very gently until the mixture begins to thicken. Stir in the ground almonds and almond essence. Cover the jam and lemon curd with this mixture. Bake at 220°C (gas mark 7) for 10 minutes, then lower the oven temperature to 180°C (gas mark 4) for 10 minutes and lower it again to 150°C (gas mark 2) for 10-15 minutes until the filling is set and golden brown.

Teas are served by the knot garden.

bakewell tart

This is the recipe I use most often for open days. Made in an oblong tin, it is easy to cut into portions. It is slightly less messy to eat with the fingers than the puff pastry version.

shortcrust pastry – *made in food processor with:*
6 oz (175 g) selfraising flour

Top: Argyranthemum frutescens.
Bottom: Papaver rhoeas 'Shirley Series'.

3-4 oz (75-110 g) margarine and lard mixed
pinch of salt
1¹/₂ tablespoons cold water

filling
6 oz (175 g) butter
6 oz (175 g) caster sugar
3 eggs, beaten
1 tablespoon ground almonds
almond essence
strawberry jam and good lemon curd

7 x 11 x 1 inch (18 x 28 x 2.5 cm) tin

Line the tin with pastry and cover the base with a thin layer of jam and lemon curd. Cream the butter and sugar. Beat in the eggs. Add the ground almonds and almond essence. Spoon the creamed mixture over the jam and lemon curd and bake at 200°C (gas mark 6) for 15 minutes; turn the temperature down to 150°C (gas mark 2) and continue cooking until the filling is set and browned. If necessary turn the temperature down again if the tart is browning too rapidly.

sponge cake

As these sponge cakes are so easy to make in a food processor, I make lots and freeze them. The flavourings can be varied, and these cakes also make excellent desserts, flavoured with vanilla and filled with whipped cream and fresh strawberries.

6 oz (175 g) margarine at room temperature
6 oz (175 g) caster sugar
6 oz (175 g) self-raising flour
1 rounded teaspoon baking powder
3 eggs
flavouring (either a few drops vanilla essence, or coffee – 1 level tablespoon dissolved in hot water
– or cocoa – 1 level tablespoon mixed to a paste with hot water)

two 7 inch (18 cm) greased sandwich cake tins

Put all the ingredients in the food processor and whisk until a smooth mixture is produced. Divide the mixture into the cake tins and bake at 180°C (gas mark 4) for 25-30 minutes until firm but still spongy to the touch.

Turn onto cooling trays and leave to cool.

Sandwich together with jam, lemon curd or butter cream filling according to the flavouring used. Home-made strawberry conserve (see above) is also a delicious filling.

lemon cake

This cake has a refreshing combination of sweetness and sharpness which is very welcome on a warm summer's day.

2 eggs, plus their combined weight (always check this as they do vary) in each of butter, sugar and self-raising flour
1 tablespoon ground almonds
1 tablespoon good lemon curd
grated rind 1 lemon, plus its juice
caster sugar

a 2 lb (900 g) loaf tin, greased and base-lined

Cream the butter and sugar and add the beaten eggs, a small amount at a time. Mix in the ground almonds, lemon curd and grated lemon rind. Fold in the flour. Spoon the mixture into the tin. Bake at 150°C (gas mark 2) for 40-45 minutes until firm and golden brown. When the cake is cool, gently spoon over the juice of 1 lemon mixed with 4 teaspoons of caster sugar.

Some hot gardening gossip is exchanged over tea.

145

Geranium oxonianum 'Sherwood'.

date and walnut loaf

This is an old favourite. I was given the recipe 50 years ago by a fellow Barnardo's organiser. We used to make it for coffee mornings then, but with its relatively low fat content and the healthy dried fruit and nuts, I feel it deserves a fashionable come-back.

8 oz (225 g) plain flour
1 oz (25 g) margarine
¹/₂ teaspoon salt
1 cup boiling water
¹/₂ teaspoon bicarbonate of soda
¹/₂ lb (225 g) chopped dates
2 oz (50 g) walnuts
1 large egg
4 oz (110 g) sugar
1 teaspoon baking powder

a 2 lb (900 g) loaf tin, greased and base-lined

Rub the margarine into the flour and salt in a large bowl. Dissolve the bicarbonate of soda in boiling water and pour over the dates and walnuts in another bowl. Leave for 20 minutes.

Add the sugar and baking powder to the flour and margarine mixture.

Add the date and walnut mixture and beaten egg. Mix well. Put into the loaf tin. Bake at 150°C (gas mark 2) for 1-1¹/₂ hours.

Serve sliced and – if you don't take low-fat too seriously – buttered.

hazelnut cookies

4 oz (110 g) margarine
4 oz (110 g) caster sugar
5 oz (150 g) self-raising flour
1 teaspoonful coffee essence (or instant coffee dissolved in 1 teaspoonful water)
3 oz (75 g) hazelnuts finely chopped (I put them in a plastic bag and crush them with a rolling pin)

Cream the margarine and sugar. Add the coffee essence, hazelnuts and flour. Form into walnut-sized balls. Place on a baking tray lined with non-stick silicone baking parchment. Bake at 150°C (gas mark 2) for 15-20 minutes until golden brown. Cool slightly before removing to a cooling tray.

fruit cake

This is best made a fortnight before you need it since it improves with keeping. This brings it closer to the gorgeous soggy texture I remember from Aunt Bea's fruit cakes.

Digitalis purpurea

She made hers in the Aga, and I'm sorry that we no longer have one.

8 oz (225 g) plain flour
8 oz (225 g) butter
8 oz (225 g) soft brown sugar
6 eggs, beaten
2 lb (900 g) mixed dried fruit
4 oz (110 g) glacé cherries
4 oz (110 g) flaked almonds
¹/₂ teaspoon bicarbonate of soda
pinch of salt
¹/₂ teaspoon mixed spice
grated rind of 1 orange and 1 lemon

a 2 lb (900 g) loaf tin, or 2 x 1 lb (450 g) tins, greased and base-lined

Cream the butter and sugar; gradually add the beaten eggs. Sieve the dry ingredients and add the grated rinds. Carefully fold the dry ingredients and fruit into the creamed mixture. If the mixture seems too stiff (it should be a soft dropping consistency) add a drop of milk.

Put the mixture into the loaf tin or 2 x 1 lb (450 g) tins and bake at 140°C (gas mark 1) for approximately 3 hours (less for the smaller cakes) until firm to the touch.

Remove from the tin when cold. Wrap in greaseproof paper and foil and store for at least two weeks before using.

drinks

These recipes are for simple country drinks that will store for weeks but are so delicious – especially in hot weather – that they never last long.

lemonade

juice and rind of 6 lemons
4 lb (1.8 kg) granulated sugar
4 pints (2.25 litres) boiling water
2 oz (50 g) epsom salts
2 oz (50 g) citric acid
2 oz (50 g) tartaric acid

Put grated lemon rind, juice, sugar and epsom salts and the acids into a large bowl and pour boiling water over the mixture, stirring well. Leave to cool. Pour into clean bottles. Dilute to taste.

elderflower cordial

20 heads of elderflowers (they must be dry)
3 to 5 lb (1.35-2.25 kg) sugar, depending on taste
3 pints (1.75 litres) cold boiled water
3 oz (75 g) tartaric acid
2 lemons, sliced

Put all the ingredients together in a large bowl and leave for 24 hours. Stir frequently to dissolve the sugar. Strain and pour into either glass or plastic bottles. Dilute to taste. Will keep for one year.

elderflower champagne

2 heads of elderflowers
8 pints (4.5 litres) cold water
1 lemon
1¹/₂ lb (700 g) granulated sugar
2 tablespoons white vinegar

Put flowers, sugar and vinegar into a large bowl. Squeeze the lemon and add juice and rind cut into four quarters. Pour on the cold water. Leave covered for 24 hours. Stir occasionally to dissolve the sugar. Strain and bottle, using screw-top plastic bottles. Keep for two weeks before using. The bottles may start to bulge as the drink ferments, so open with care.

lunches and suppers

salmon

If you own or can borrow a fish kettle, salmon is a very easy dish to prepare for a summer lunch or dinner. Wash and gut the salmon and place it on the trivet in the fish kettle. Cover it with cold water, or a mixture of cold water and white wine, and add twelve whole black peppercorns, a bay leaf, and a lemon cut into slices. Bring to boiling point as slowly and gently as possible, then take off the heat and leave the salmon to cool in the liquor.

A 6 lb (2.7 kg) salmon will serve about 30 people for a buffet meal.

chicken & orange rice salad

This comes from a book called 'Super Scoff', which I saw reviewed in a Daily Telegraph food column in 1970. It contains so many recipes which I like that it has fallen

Iris.

Top: Inula hookeri.
Bottom: Lysimachia punctata.

to pieces and I now keep the dog-eared pages in a plastic bag.

the chicken

1 4-5 lb (1.8-2.25 kg) chicken, roasted in foil, and cut into small pieces
1 medium onion, finely chopped
1 clove of garlic
1 green pepper
2 oz (50 g) sliced mushrooms
10 fluid oz (275 ml) mayonnaise
1 tablespoon cream
1 oz grated almonds
salt and pepper
tabasco
butter
chopped parsley

the orange rice salad

12 oz (350 g) patna rice
salt
5-6 tablespoons orange juice
finely grated rind of half an orange
finely cut strips of rind of half an orange

Gently fry the chopped onion and crushed garlic in a little butter until soft. Cut the pepper into thin strips and plunge into boiling water for one minute, then add to the onions with the mushrooms and cook for one minute. Cool. Stir the chicken and onion mixture into the mayonnaise with a little cream, tabasco and seasoning. Cook the rice and half of the orange rind in boiling salted water. Drain and cool. Stir in orange juice and seasoning. Arrange rice round the edge of a large serving dish. Put the chicken mixture in the centre, sprinkle with almonds and chopped parsley. Boil remaining strips of orange peel in water for 5 minutes, drain, cool and use to decorate the rice. Serves 8 to 10.

ham

It is worth cooking your own ham using this method; a little fiddlier than the salmon, but again, something that can be prepared well in advance, and needs only some new potatoes and green salad to accompany it. I usually buy a 7-8 lbs (3-3.5 kg) joint and soak it overnight in water to remove the salt. Cover it with fresh cold water in a large pan, bring very slowly to a simmer, and poach very gently for one hour. Pour off half the liquid, and add the same amount of pineapple juice to make up the quantity of liquid. Bring to a simmer and poach for a further hour, again very gently. Then remove from the stove and wrap the saucepan tightly in an old towel, so that the ham can continue to cook in its own heat. When cold, take the skin off the joint and score the fat with a sharp knife in criss-cross diamond shapes. Stick a clove into each diamond, and smear the joint with a paste made of 1 tablespoon mustard mixed with 1 tablespoon soft brown sugar. Bake in a hot oven at 220° C (gas mark 7) for about 20 minutes until well browned. A ham this size will feed about 25 to 30 people.

salmon mousse

This easy mousse, and the following recipe for devilled egg mousse, can be used as a light main course for lunch, or as a starter for a larger meal.

> *8 oz (225 g) tin salmon (preferably red)*
> *¹/₄ pint (150 ml) mayonnaise (3 heaped tablespoons)*
> *¹/₄ pint (150 ml) double cream*
> *4 level teaspoons gelatine*
> *1 tablespoon lemon juice*
> *a few drops of tabasco*
> *salt and pepper*

Flake the salmon, mix with the mayonnaise. Whip the cream, fold into the salmon mixture. Dissolve the gelatine in the lemon juice and fold into the mousse. Season. Pour into a lightly oiled mould to set.

devilled egg mousse

This mousse is light in texture but rich in its flavouring. It is substantial enough to stand alone but is also good as a starter.

> *8 hard-boiled eggs*
> *¹/₂ pint (275 ml) mayonnaise*
> *¹/₂ pint (275 ml) béchamel sauce (see below)*
> *4 level teaspoons gelatine dissolved in 2 tablespoons stock or water*
> *¹/₄ pint (150 ml) double cream*
> *cayenne pepper*
> *devil sauce (see below)*

Start by making the béchamel sauce, with:

> *1 oz (25 g) butter*
> *1 oz (25 g) plain flour*
> *¹/₂ pint (275 ml) liquid (stock and wine, or milk, stock and wine) infused for 20 minutes with small pieces of carrot, celery, and onion; 4 black peppercorns, a small bayleaf and a pinch of mace; add salt to taste*

Top: Hemerocallis.
Bottom: Argyranthemum.

Top: Agapanthus.
Bottom: Muscari armeniacum.

Make as for a basic roux sauce, and leave to cool.

Then make up the devil sauce, with:

1 cup canned chopped tomatoes
pinch of sugar
¹/₂ garlic clove, crushed
2 tablespoons olive oil
1 dessertspoon vinegar
1 tablespoon Worcester Sauce
1 dessertspoon tomato ketchup
salt, pepper and a good pinch of dry mustard powder

a lightly oiled 2 pint (1.2 litre) ring mould or a 7 inch (18cm) cake tin

Mix all the ingredients together in a saucepan and cook slowly until thick and pulpy. Cool and put to one side.

Finely chop the hard-boiled eggs. Stir the mayonnaise into the béchamel sauce, and stir in the dissolved gelatine.

Fold in the chopped eggs and the cream and season well. Pour the mixture into the mould or tin. Leave to set.

Turn out the mousse, decorate with cucumber and tomatoes and pour some sauce round the edge. Serve with the remaining sauce. Serves 8 to 10 people.

foolproof meringues

4 egg whites, at least a week old
8 oz (225 g) caster sugar

Meringues are not difficult, but it's reassuring to know a foolproof way of making them. I make these meringues two or three days before I need them and store them unfilled in an airtight tin. Having once forgotten about a batch, I can vouch that they can remain in perfect condition for five weeks.

Prepare two baking sheets by lining with non-stick baking paper, or lightly oil the sheets and dredge with plain flour, shaking to distribute the flour evenly.

In a clean, dry bowl whisk the egg whites until they are very stiff and smooth. I use a balloon whisk on my electric mixer for this. If you dare, turn the bowl upside down, and if the egg whites remain in the bowl they are the correct consistency.

For each egg white used, add in 1 teaspoon of sugar (that is, 4 teaspoons for this quantity) and whisk for 1 minute. Fold in the remaining sugar with a large metal spoon (it is important to fold, not mix). Spoon the mixture (using either a dessertspoon or a tablespoon, depending on the size of meringue you require) onto the prepared trays, spacing about ½ inch (1cm) apart. Alternatively the mixture can be piped onto the trays using a meringue piping nozzle and a large fabric piping bag. Dredge with a little caster sugar and leave 1 minute to allow the sugar to soften slightly: this will give a crystallised appearance to the finished meringue.

Bake for 1 hour at 140°C, (gas mark 1) changing the trays round after half an hour – this is not usually necessary in a fan assisted oven. After 1 hour, remove the trays from the oven and carefully lift each meringue from the tray, making a small hole on the underside with a sharp knife (this lets out any steam). Put the meringues back on the trays, laying them on their sides to dry, and return to the oven for 20 – 30 minutes. Cool on a wire rack. Store until required or sandwich together with whipped cream and use within 1-2 hours after filling.

Makes 30 meringue halves, that is 15 filled meringues.

Geranium phaeum.

Gill Buck, 1998.

11 gardening for wrinklies

As the gardener grows older, aches and pains become more insistent. But you now have the advantage of years of experience, and you are rewarded by seeing the results of past efforts. The garden can be a sanctuary at times of crisis, and a place of healing. Even as you come to terms with the ending of your intervention in nature, dreams of future projects never cease.

It may seem a little odd to begin my final chapter with a recipe for an aromatherapy oil for arthritic joints. However, the sad fact is that most of us only get the time to garden seriously when our bodies are already in decline.

The aches may become more insistent each year, but there are advantages to being an ageing gardener. Each season adds to the accumulation of knowledge and experience which makes gardening an activity of ever deepening richness. My garden gives me a sense of the passing of time, as I see plantings designed a few years earlier grow to maturity. I will probably not see some of my trees reach their full height, but I like to think that something I planted may be appreciated by somebody who is not yet born.

Gardens do not create themselves. They are the result of our intervention, and rely on our constant effort. As a child, my grandfather's garden seemed to be something made for all time. After his death it continued to flourish in the hands of my aunt and uncle. But time caught up with them, and after they left the house for a retirement flat, it stood empty until the tide of new housing from an expanding Dronfield finally washed over it and the garden was filled with blocks of flats. Awaiting redevelopment, dereliction swept through the garden almost as fast as through the vandalised house. Within a year or two the garden was suffocated by weeds, and there was no sign of the orderly rows of vegetables and bedding plants, and the neatly pruned roses that created its distinctive atmosphere. I am keenly aware that the garden at Fanshawe Gate may have its roots in many years of work and planning, but that its attractiveness to a visitor depends on how much work we are able to put in each day of the current season.

However, even at times when we are not able to do so much and the garden becomes unkempt, it still means a great deal to me because of my personal links with many of the plants. I never look at plants with the eye of a horticulturalist or a garden designer, but with thoughts about the person who gave them to me, or the place where I found them. Perhaps this is why the garden has been a place of solace at the most difficult time of my life.

We were very busy with garden openings during the summer of 1997, and I ignored an occasional strange feeling in my throat. Even when I started to have difficulty swallowing, I decided that this was unlikely to be serious; the pensioner's equivalent of the 'growing pains' which I used to diagnose in my children. It was a cold shock when,

aromatherapy oil for arthritic joints

This oil will ease discomfort in your thumbs, wrists and knees. Massaged into the creaking area, it produces a lovely warm feeling, and it smells delicious.

To a base of 100mls of sweet almond oil add:

10 drops lavender oil
10 drops marjoram oil
10 drops juniper oil
4 drops ginger oil
4 drops cedarwood oil

Shake all the ingredients together in a bottle, label, and keep out of sunlight. Shake it well again before use. Perhaps it is wise to test some on a small area of skin first, as these oils are rather powerful.

as the visiting season drew to a close and I finally found time for a check-up, I learned that cancer had spread through my oesophagus. A major operation followed within a few days. I lay in hospital looking at the cards and flowers, drawing daily more strength and comfort from the people who prayed with me and for me. But I had to come to terms with the knowledge that I would not be able to dig or lift for a long time. Perhaps I would never regain the ability to bend down to weed or to pick something off the ground without discomfort.

I knew that Mark and John Pitts would put the garden to bed for the winter, and my friend and Plant Aid colleague, John Simcox, was preparing to lift the pelargoniums and fuchsias, taking cuttings ready for the next summer. When I heard that John Simcox had managed to lift my prized 'Vancouver Centennial' pelargonium just before the first frost, and I found the energy to be deeply grateful, I knew that my recovery had begun.

For anyone recovering from a serious illness or a setback in their life, or simply suffering dismay at the effects of the passing years, I recommend retreating to a sanctuary. In my case this meant the potting shed and the greenhouse. Throughout the winter months following my operation I worked steadily at the potting bench, pricking out seedlings and potting on cuttings. The potting shed was warm and cosy, and even the feeblest ray of winter sun would heat the greenhouse. I listened to the radio and thought about the coming spring. I looked at the first snowdrops, crocuses and miniature daffodils as if for the first time. I felt the rising excitement of warmer sun, lighter nights and brightening birdsong more keenly than ever before. I was determined that life would carry on as normal, so in the summer of 1998, with a great deal of help from our family and friends, the garden opened again. It was a record year for visitors and plant sales.

At the end of that season I did not feel my usual sadness at the beginning of autumn. I used to dread the melancholy effect on me of fading, dying flowers, dropping leaves, and the dull dampness of the Pennine weather. This time I noticed the warm autumn colours, the stillness, and the glistening cobwebs on the yew trees. I even looked forward to winter, thinking about frosted twigs, and snow capping the gateposts and topiary. My attitude to the dead time of the year has changed for ever. It is only one part of God's cycle – a starkly beautiful one at that – and it will return to life.

Three years later, I have learned to dig and weed in the garden again by bending my knees and keeping my back straight. I needed no further treatment or aftercare; I was very fortunate.

I have resumed my old habit of planning and dreaming. No doubt I should be thinking about how to create a lower maintenance garden, now that John and I are both in our seventies, but new ideas keep bubbling up.

A project I have been thinking over for some time is the creation of a *parterre* or low maze in the upper courtyard, with an armillary at its centre. I imagined it as a way of marking the new millennium. The rest of the family are trying to dissuade me, with objections ranging from the practical – 'where will you hang out the washing?' – to the impertinent – 'there won't be room to turn the hearse round'. We shall see.

Another idea for the future is to make more of the orchard and the vegetable garden, areas which are much as they were in 1959, except that the fruit trees are forty years older. I would like to replace them with new trees, and I am researching which of the old varieties, with their subtle flavours, will grow well in this region. I can also imagine the orchard organised more formally, with a vine walkway clothed in golden hop – *Humulus lupulus* 'Aureus' – and the contrasting plum-coloured foliage of *Vitis vinifera* 'Purpurea'. Perhaps I could grow a romantic camomile seat at the end of the walkway? And how about some old-fashioned conical beehives? As for the vegetable garden, the rest of my dream is to create a proper *potager*; to replace the utilitarian straight rows of produce with vegetables, fruit and flowers, all interplanted with each other in a way my grandfather would have regarded as frivolous.

Even if these dreams never become reality, I cannot imagine a time when I no longer have projects, schemes and fantasies for the garden. It still seems miraculous to have come through my illness with my hopes for the future intact. My gratitude for this goes to the Oesophageal Patients Association, who gave me precious support in the immediate aftermath, and continue to do so. Also, although I did not need a Macmillan cancer nurse, I know many people whose illness would have been hard to bear without them. When I send contributions from our open days to these two charities, I do so with deeply heartfelt thanks.

My greatest fortune of all is to have been the custodian of Fanshawe Gate for most of my gardening life. Not only that, but also to have shared that gardening life with my family and friends, who will probably never know quite how much it has all meant to me.

editor **nicola ball**
design **lindy payling**
photography **mark ramsden**
additional photography **lu jeffery, sean hoyland, john pitts**
garden plans **rachel mcqueen**
illustrations **delys fiddes, gill buck, myra powell**
publicity **integra communications**

I am very grateful to all the people, especially Lindy Payling, Nicola Ball, and the Grafika team, who volunteered their time and professional skills to produce this book, with the aim of supporting the two charities.

I would like to thank Lu Jeffery, who very kindly gave us permission to use some of her pictures. She took the picture on the jacket cover, and the one at the beginning of the chapter on Quiet Corners. Sean Hoyland is another professional photographer who generously took photographs for the chapters on Potting Sheds and Open Days.

Delys Fiddes has been a family friend for many years, but I don't think any of us had realised the depth of her artistic skills. She responded with grace and astonishing patience to some unreasonably last-minute requests for illustrations.

I am also indebted to the Sheffield University of the Third Age, members of whose sketching group lent their drawings and paintings for reproduction in the book. We always enjoy their visits to Fanshawe Gate, and hope they will continue to find artistic inspiration here. Other illustrations are from our own collection. We have requested permission to use Roy Gender's photographs, and the quotation from Constance Spry's book.

Some of the professional contributors to the book have also been hard workers in the garden at Fanshawe Gate, none more so than Mark Ramsden. For help beyond the call of duty I should mention Rachel McQueen, who, in addition to preparing all the garden plans, took time off from her horticultural studies to save our borders from ground elder.

We have had invaluable help from Barbara Jones, Clare and Alan Dobie, and from Pauline Climpson of the Hallamshire Press. No doubt if we had taken even more of their time we would have avoided all sorts of mistakes. Naturally, any errors that remain are our responsibility alone.

Cynthia Ramsden

acknowledgements

autumn

'The History of the Fanshawe Family', H.C. Fanshawe C.S.I.
pub. Andrew Reid and Company Limited, 1927

'The Memoirs of Ann Lady Fanshawe'
pub. John Lane The Bodley Head, 1907

'Incunabula of Sheffield History', T. Walter Hall
pub. J.W. Northend Ltd, 1937

'I Bought a Farm', Roy Genders
pub. The Worcester Press, 1948

'Chantrey Land', Harold Armitage
pub. Sampson Low, Marston & Company, 1910

'How to do the Flowers', Constance Spry
pub. Atlantis Publishing Company

My copy is undated but seems to have been written just after the Second World War. I was struck by the following observation she makes:

'Many a man and woman during the bad and violent years that have fallen to us have found, through flowers and gardens, solace from worry and strained nerves and escape from sordidness and anxiety. Allotments really took hold of us during the 1914-1918 war and many learned for the first time the healing that comes through working in the soil and the joy and elation that is to be found in the miracle of growing a plant from seed'.

'Super Scoff'
pub. The Warwickshire Association of Youth Clubs, 1970

My recipe is based on the one for Cold Chicken and Orange Rice Salad given by Mrs M.G. Harwood. I think she would be amused to know how many times it has appeared on our table.

bibliography

'I'm a traditionalist at heart, and I love the way that they have so sympathetically brought Fanshawe Gate back to its former glory, and given it a feeling of eternity.' Jill Bethell

GARDEN *Tales*

by Cynthia Ramsden

The new book about the garden at Fanshawe Gate Hall, published in 2009.

'When I came to the end of my first book, 'A Garden in my Life', in 2001, I could not resist writing about the dreams I had for further development of the garden at Fanshawe Gate Hall. It seemed like tempting fate. However, I'm delighted to say that, eight years later, the most ambitious plans have become reality...'

So begins 'Garden Tales', Cynthia Ramsden's enchanting sequel to 'A Garden in my Life', which brings her readers up to date with how the garden has developed in the first years of the twenty-first century.

Since 1994, Cynthia and John Ramsden have opened their garden each summer to an increasingly appreciative public, raising many thousands of pounds for various charities. In 2009, a year when 2,500 people visited the garden, Cynthia and John received the National Gardens Scheme Exceptional Service award, the first garden owners to be honoured in this way.

'Garden Tales' goes behind the scenes at Fanshawe Gate Hall, as gardeners, designers, builders, artists, volunteers and visitors talk about their own lives, and what brings them back, year after year, to this enchanting spot on the edge of the Peak District National Park.

I enjoy working at Fanshawe Gate: it's a delightful place. I've never worked anywhere else where, no matter what the weather, you can always find a nice, quiet corner; somewhere pleasant and peaceful to work in.

Peter Wolfendale

Sometimes I come home after an open day thinking, 'Oh my back! My legs! My knees!' I'm shattered, but I still can't wait for next week. Gail Wheelhouse

Narrated in the words of a host of fascinating characters, 'Garden Tales' offers delightful insights into those very English pastimes of gardening and garden visiting. But it is not just a book about a garden, for the stories told by its many contributors (and one cockerel) also give some moving – and amusing – glimpses of the lives we lead now.

'When we open our gardens, we share a part of our lives with other people. What characterises the National Gardens Scheme is the generosity of garden visitors, owners and volunteers. The same spirit of generosity shines through the accounts in this book, as each person shares their life with us, the readers. Impressive, inspiring, and hopeful, what they have to say about gardening and living – growing up as well as growing old – is a real treat.'

From the Foreword by Penny Snell, Chairman of the National Gardens Scheme

'Garden Tales' can be ordered online at **www.fanshawegate.com** or from the publishers, Grafika Limited (call 01629 813300 for details). 'Garden Tales' costs £16.99, including post and packing. It is also available in a boxed set with 'A Garden in my Life' for the special offer price of £32, including post and packing – an ideal gift for garden enthusiasts.

Sales of the First Edition of 'A Garden in my Life' raised £8,000 for Macmillan Cancer Support and the Oesophageal Patients Association. Profits from sales of the Second Edition of 'A Garden in my Life' and of 'Garden Tales', will also be donated to these charities, as well as to the other principal charities supported by the National Gardens Scheme: Marie Curie Cancer Care, Help the Hospices, and Crossroads – Caring for Carers.

Garden Open Days

The garden at Fanshawe Gate Hall will be open under the National Gardens Scheme in June and July 2010. Private group visits are also welcome by appointment during June and July; please call 0114 289 0391.

ngs gardens open for charity
Registered Charity No.1112664

FANSHAWE GATE HALL

The Oesophageal Patients Association
Registered Charity No.1062461